GO ALL IN

COLIN YURCISIN

GO ALL IN

HOW I WENT FROM
50K IN DEBT AT 23 TO
MULTIMILLIONAIRE BY 24

LIONCREST
PUBLISHING

GO ALL IN

How I Went from 50K in Debt at 23 to Multimillionaire by 24

ISBN   978-1-5445-3797-9   *Hardcover*
       978-1-5445-3798-6   *Paperback*
       978-1-5445-3799-3   *Ebook*
       978-1-5445-3851-8   *Audiobook*

Dedicated to Mom and Dad.

CONTENTS

INTRODUCTION

THE NEW AMERICAN DREAM

Today, I sit here in my three-million dollar apartment, seventy-three floors above the Atlantic Ocean. From my home office, I run three successful seven- and eight-figure businesses. I have millions in Bitcoin, own real estate, recently helped my mother retire, and frequently take my family on dream vacations to places like Bora Bora. I am surrounded by incredible people on a daily basis and live with the woman of my dreams. Sounds like a fairy tale, right?

Well, my life wasn't always like this. Only three years ago, I was $50,000 in debt. I was twenty-three years old, scared, lost, and confused about what to do and where to go in my life. I had a business degree and a job, but I had no idea where I was going or, more importantly, *why*.

Today I can proudly say that I know my "why." I have found my purpose, and I am on my right path. Was it easy? No. Did I stray from the path repeatedly to get here? Abso-fucking-lutly.

This book is many things: my story; a guidebook for anyone looking to find more meaning, fulfillment, and success in their lives; and a manifesto to express my truth. And that truth is that in this life, nothing is more important than finding your purpose and then going *all in* to fulfill it.

This book is for anyone who wants to live an extraordinary life—a life that is filled with adventure, laughter, travel, money, success, love, joy, and freedom. It is also for anyone who is tired of the mundane, boring, and repetitive structure that society has led us to believe is "normal." And it is for those who are ready to break out of "The Matrix" and become a real player in this game called **life**.

This book will take you on a journey through my life, but my story is not all that different from most people's stories. It is the story of a little boy who had access to infinite intelligence but who faced such great resistance—both from the voices of others and the voices within himself—that he temporarily lost his way. It is the brutally honest, behind-the-scenes story of how I found my way back to my true self and went on to create the life of my dreams from scratch. More importantly, it is the story of how *you* can do it too.

I firmly believe that there are millions of people out there just like me who have lost sight of the reason why they were put on this earth. With this book, I hope to help you find your way back to your purpose, and back to your path, so that by the end, you will finally understand how going *all in* will lead you to your best life.

Are you ready?

ONE

BE A
CREATOR

WAS BORN IN NEW JERSEY. MY MOM AND DAD'S FAM-
ily have always lived in the Garden State, and to this day,
my mom's mom lives in Mount Laurel, which is in South
Jersey, and my dad's mom lives in Roselle Park, which
is in North Jersey, only forty minutes from New York City.
No one in my family ever ventured outside of Jersey. I don't
know if it was a fear thing, a family thing, or the fact that
they actually enjoyed five months of freezing cold weather
every year and insane property taxes, but whatever the reason, they stayed.

Ever since I was a kid, I've been wildly imaginative. When
I was four years old, I decided I was the CEO of a company

called Calendana. I'm guessing it was a version of my name with a sort of twist on the end? According to my mom, I'd say stuff like, "My assistant Ashley is bringing hot dogs for all the workers today!"

She would ask me, "What does your business sell, Colin?" and I would reply, "Growing hair medicine! Old men rub it on their heads and it makes their hair grow!"

At the time, I was obsessed with bald people; I was fascinated by their shiny heads. One day while I was watching TV, a commercial came on for some hair growth medicine. Bald people could rub this goo on their scalps, and like magic, they would have a full head of hair after a few applications. I was blown away.

I even had the location of my business all figured out. One time we went on a trip to Baltimore Harbor, Maryland, where I pointed to a building and said, "Look! That's where my office Calendana was before it burnt down!" Yes, I had offices in different states, sold hair growth medicine, and fed my employees hot dogs, all at the age of four.

For my next entrepreneurial venture, at the age of six, I got into the publishing business. Seriously. I was a big fan of Captain Underpants, and then I discovered comic books and became obsessed with them, too. Naturally, I decided to become a comic book author myself. I sat in my room all day, folding sheets of printer paper in half and stapling them down the creased line. I proceeded to fill the book with my own comics.

Not only was I quite creative at this young age, but I was also hungry for cash. As soon as I finished a comic book, I put a price tag on it, down in the bottom right corner. Initially, I sold them for fifty cents, but the price soon went up to four dollars. After pricing the book, I began the marketing phase, running downstairs and bringing my newly minted comic book to my mom: "Mom! Look! I made this one especially for you! And it's only four dollars!" It was an easy sale. I'd then take the cash and coins up to my room and put them in my piggy bank.

Then there were the Legos. Whenever I got a new set, I followed the instructions and built whatever it was: a Harry Potter scene, a battleship, whatever. Then I tore the Legos apart and made my own original contraption with all of the pieces. That was my favorite part, and I could get lost in it for hours.

There were zero creative types or entrepreneurs in my immediate family; everyone was a corporate ladder climber. My father was a sales manager, and a few years after I was born, my mother quit her job to raise me full-time. My dad had to travel for work almost every week, so she was needed at home. Overall, I had a happy, loving childhood.

My childhood teachers figured out pretty early on that something was not quite right with me. My imagination wasn't just limited to my business ideas or the stories I would tell my family. I shared it with all of my classmates, too.

"My dad and I ripped snowmobiles all through the neighborhood during winter break!"

This was a lie—we didn't own any snowmobiles, nor had I ever been on one. My imagination and creativity were always in high gear, but the environment I lived in had no patience for it. If you think about it, most kids' environments don't. My teacher got so tired of me ignoring her when she called on me in class (only because my head was in the clouds) that she called a meeting with my mom. They decided I should see a doctor, and pretty soon I was diagnosed with ADHD. My mom never filled the prescription for Focalin because she had researched it and knew about all of the negative side effects. Instead, she emphasized the importance of paying attention and participating in class. I did my best to improve but, over time, the problems got worse.

My elementary school was in Hightstown, a multiethnic, urban neighborhood in the center of East Windsor, the more upscale suburb that surrounded it. We had a diverse group of kids in my school—Black, Hispanic, Asian, Indian, and White. One of my first friends was a kid named Michael.

Every day, we walked past the projects on our way home from school to get to his house, where we played Halo, RuneScape, and Yu-Gi-Oh cards. He had a whole video game lair on the third floor of his house, which was like heaven to me. Michael was adopted, and he used to angrily scream at his parents all the time, curse at them, and tell them stuff like "fuck off" and "go away."

Then there was Kenny, who invited me over for a playdate and showed me porn for the first time. I was nine. I ended up getting in big trouble for that with my parents and eventually wasn't allowed to play with Kenny anymore, but by then it was too late. I was hooked. I had already visited tons of sites early in the morning before my parents woke up. I was mortified when my parents found out what I'd been using their computer for. I felt a deep sense of shame for the first time in my life. I couldn't take it, so I blamed it all on Kenny, claiming that he must have browsed those sites when he was over at our house.

The point is, in all of these various ways, my childhood environment began to strip my innocence away at an early age. I'm not saying that this could have been prevented. People from all walks of life are exposed to the harsh realities of the world through their childhoods in many different ways.

Right before fifth grade, my dad got promoted, so we moved on up to Robbinsville. It was filled with much wealthier people and had a very different vibe from East Windsor. In Robbinsville, everybody knew everything about everybody else. There were BMWs, soccer moms, alcoholics, divorcées, and all the other things you'd expect to find in a typical upper-class suburban town. High school sports were the main topic of conversation until it was time to brag about where your kid was going to college. Most of the homes in this neighborhood had pools and an acre of land. My house had a huge hill in the backyard that was perfect for snowboarding.

I became best friends with Dante and Mario, two Italian brothers who lived a few houses away from us. They were always fighting in a hilarious way. Dante was a huge guy. He played football and was a big joker. He was a year older than me, and Mario, who also cracked me up, was two years younger than me. We all clicked, and for a while, we were three peas in a pod. We hung out and played video games or went swimming in their pool. One day, while searching the web, we came across something called YouTube. It was 2006, and YouTube had only been around for a year. We became obsessed. We watched funny videos online for hours on end, and one day, we decided it would be fun to create some videos of our own.

We created a YouTube channel, "Codeblack23." I have no idea where the name came from; we just thought it sounded cool, and from that day on we became YouTubers. I borrowed my mom's camera, and after posting a few videos, we had our first major hit. It was a video of me levitating, which was a very simple magic trick: all you have to do is position yourself a certain way in front of the camera and push up on your toes on one foot, and cover that foot with your other foot. It looks like you're floating. The video went viral, with more than 50,000 views, which was a lot back then, especially for three kids just messing around. We were hooked, and I was having the time of my life.

Throughout the summer, I continued to film Dante and Mario doing little comedy skits. We could do this for hours. Then, I took the videos home to edit them. We watched a lot of Smosh videos (the biggest YouTubers at the time) to get ideas, but for the most part, filming and editing YouTube videos came naturally to me and felt effortless. Maybe it was because my grandpa was a photographer, so it ran in my blood. And the funny thing is, the people around us had no idea what we were doing. In fact, nobody even knew what YouTube was. Our parents thought we were just playing around with the camera.

One summer day, Mario, Dante, our other friend Dom, and I headed to the river behind our house in the woods and filmed a three-hour parkour YouTube video of us jumping over trees and diving into the river. We went *all in* and felt like it was our best work yet. But when I went home to upload the video into the computer to edit it, there was a memory card malfunction and all of the footage was unreadable. I was horrified. We were all devastated, and Mario and Dante were angry at me for losing all of our hard work. After that, we stopped posting together on our channel.

Fifth grade started at my new school. Although my parents wanted me to repeat the fourth grade due to my concentration issues, my IQ scored too high for the school to let me repeat. Since I was the new kid, the girls seemed to like me, maybe because I was different from the rest of the kids. But of course, this caused jealousy from the other guys. One day a kid named Ryan told everyone he was going to fight me after school because of a girl named Nicole, who I was supposedly flirting with in class. I was scared shitless. I had never fought anyone before. The rumors flew around the school all day. When the final bell rang, we all walked out to the field by the buses for the big fight. Thankfully, the teachers had found out about it and were all there to break the fight up.

Fifth grade was also rough because I had some health problems. I'd always had a bad habit of eating way too much sugary cereal, and it was around this time that I developed hypoglycemia. I started shaking when my blood sugar dropped too low and would sometimes have to go to the nurse during class. This also caused me to have to go to the bathroom every twenty minutes, which was extremely embarrassing. I called it the "shaky feeling" and the "pee problem." The doctor told me to eat less sugary cereal, so I switched to Special K and Cheerios, but I sure wish he would have also told me to eat more meat, eggs, and animal fats. Unfortunately, back in those days, the FDA was telling us to follow their food pyramid scam that involved tons of carbs, saturated fats, seed oils, and processed sugar. Switching to a high protein diet would have helped me avoid a huge problem that was coming in the next few years: cystic acne.

The first kid I talked to in my homeroom class that year was Josh. He was a skateboarder, and I gravitated toward that right away. Almost instantly, I picked up a skateboard and started hanging out with the skater crew. There hadn't been any skateboarders in East Windsor, but it was huge in Robbinsville; there was even a skate park.

I went *all in*. Josh taught me the tricks and told me what kind of wheels and skater shoes to buy. Very quickly I developed a passion for skateboarding. It was artistic. It was pure freedom and creativity. It felt rebellious and exciting to skate around town and then go hit the skate park. There were no rules; you made it up as you went along. The skater crew all had hair down to their shoulders, so I grew my hair out, too. I'd put a beanie on my wet head in the morning after my shower and my hair would dry up like I had wings. I thought I looked amazing.

Unfortunately, my parents did not feel the same way about skateboarding. In fact, they didn't approve. Especially my dad, because he knew the skater kids were smoking cigarettes and weed and hanging out at the skate park all day. My dad was an athlete; he wrestled and played football and baseball in high school. He didn't even have his first drink until he was eighteen because he was so committed to sports. He wanted me to do the same, and from the moment I could walk he had me out hitting balls off the tee and throwing a football. He put me into wrestling, baseball, and flag football in middle school so I could be ready for the high school teams. I just didn't have much passion for it, nor was I that good, so it became a bit of a battle between us. He still let me skateboard, but it had to be after wrestling and baseball. He would say, "When you're done with practice, you can go home and do whatever the hell you want."

Every day after school, I had to go to wrestling practice in the cafeteria for three hours. Then there was baseball. My dad was the baseball coach, so of course, he always made me practice more than anyone else. He often told me to "put down the skateboard" because we were heading to the field to hit balls or field grounders. I went along with it because I never wanted to disrespect my dad, but deep down I couldn't wait to get back to skating.

When it came to baseball and wrestling, I always tried my best. But I was always doing it for him. At baseball practice, all of the guys talked about their favorite players, which team had won the game the previous night, and all that. They knew all the stats and the players. One day I accidentally said "New Jersey Mets" instead of "New York Mets," and immediately, everyone realized I didn't know shit about baseball, so they began to pick on me. They'd quiz me, saying the name of a city and asking me to name the team. I never got more than a couple right. It hurt my dad so badly that he started quizzing me on professional sports teams' names on the way to and from practice. It was so annoying. My heart was in skateboarding and filming, my creative outlets, which I barely had time for anymore. I couldn't have cared less about professional sports teams or what fucking city they were from.

I continued to skateboard when I could and soon realized that skateboarding was a huge trend on YouTube. I became obsessed with watching my favorite filmers and skaters, and I wanted to participate, too. So I started recording my tricks, editing them into mash-ups, and putting them on YouTube. That became my creative outlet. It was one thing to play with Legos, draw all the time, create comic books, or shoot skits of my friends being funny, but now I was sharing my real passion with the world.

I couldn't hide it anymore; skateboarding became my lifestyle. I looked up to all the older skater guys because they were so good and so cool to me. I felt proud that they let me film them. I explored the town, looking for all the best skate spots, with my skater friends. We all wore black skinny jeans and skater shoes with holes in them. The skater vibe was definitely grungy, but I loved it.

I loved that I could skateboard anywhere. It's not like a sport where you have to team up and there's a game plan. You can do whatever trick you want. You can practice flat ground or you can hit ramps. You can design your deck however you want. You can get cool wheels. But the best part was that skateboarding videos were a huge trend, and I was determined to film the best videos.

Now I was skating, filming it, putting an edit together, and launching a video on YouTube, all at twelve years old. I brought my camera everywhere.

Remember Tech Decks? Those little mini skateboards you play with your fingers? Well, I was obsessed with them, too.

As soon as I got home from my sports practices every day, I took my fingerboard and ramps to the kitchen and practiced for hours. I banged the board all over the kitchen, making so much noise that my mom would tell me to go do it in my room. But there was nothing better than the smooth surface of the granite kitchen countertop. I was, however, too afraid to fingerboard in front of my dad. I could tell he thought it was weird. When I was done with my fingerboard and ramps, I went to the garage to practice kickflips, heel flips, and tre flips on the real skateboard. I filmed everything from my skate and fingerboard sessions and then headed to my room to edit my movies on iMovie before uploading them to YouTube. I was totally immersed in the process of creating. I didn't know it at the time, but I had begun to experience a true flow state.

Still, I was the "new kid" in school, which continued to put a big target on my back. Even some of the skater kids bullied me. One day I was putting my books away in my locker when, all of a sudden, my backpack was violently pulled off my back and I ended up smacking my head on the concrete floor. I probably got a concussion and was definitely disoriented. I looked up and saw one of the kids in the skater group walking away laughing.

Things got worse when some of my skater friends found the skits I had done with Mario and Dante on YouTube and made fun of them. One day they hacked into my channel and deleted all of the videos. I was crushed. I couldn't believe how stupid I'd been when I posted those videos. I suddenly realized how silly and immature they were. From that point on, I stopped. I gave up on everything—no more skits, no more YouTube; I let it all go. I just wanted the skaters to be my friends. And it worked; they stopped bullying me after that. To them, the deleted videos were just a joke; but for me, it hurt, and it killed my inspiration for a long time. This was the point in my life when I stopped being my authentic self and began to silence the creative voice inside of me.

T W O

STICK
WITH IT

IGH SCHOOL WAS AN ENTIRELY NEW WORLD. The seniors looked so old! On the first day of school, I walked past kids who were six foot three and wore varsity jackets. They were driving, partying, having sex, and visiting colleges, and I was fascinated. They were the real deal, and I couldn't wait to be just like them.

All of my skater friends from middle school and I had the same realization—if we wanted to get laid, skateboarding had to go. And just like that, we were done with it. All thoughts of becoming a professional videographer, editor, or skateboarder went right out the window. All I wanted was to fit in, be cool, lift weights, go to parties, and get chicks. I had no interest in sports, of course, so most days when I got home from school that fall, I just played video games. I worked hard in school because I knew I had to take academics seriously if I wanted to get into a good college. I take that back. I worked somewhat hard, and always managed to get C-pluses and Bs, but that was about it.

Winter rolled around and one day, my dad came home from work, walked up to the TV where I was playing *Call of Duty: Modern Warfare*, and just shut it off, without any warning. "Get your ass off the couch," he said. "You're going to high school wrestling practice."

"Dad! I told you! I don't like wrestling; I don't want to do it!" I argued.

"I don't want to hear it. You're going."

I was terrified. High school sports were a whole different animal than the recreation-level sports I'd been playing in middle school. I would be with eighteen-year-olds. Some of them weighed 250 pounds. I was still only fourteen years old, and I was skinny. I hadn't even had my growth spurt yet. But clearly, I did not have a choice.

It was brutal. First, there was the food problem. Food is literally my favorite thing on earth, and I've always had a sweet tooth. I love all kinds of food, but now I couldn't even eat, because I had to cut my weight for wrestling. But hey, it made my dad happy and allowed me to go to parties with no questions asked. Also, it felt like a kind of rite of passage with my father. To be honest, I didn't know what I was getting myself into. Wrestling was so tough that everything else in life seemed like a joke. My coaches wanted me to cut down two weight classes so I could wrestle the smaller kids, which would give me a better chance of winning. So with this goal in mind, my days started at 5:00 a.m. Every morning I wrapped myself in plastic bags so I could go running in the freezing cold. My breakfast consisted of one scrambled egg and spinach. By 7:00 a.m., I was at school filling up a water bottle with my spit to lose extra water weight. I'd watch the other kids sitting around eating lunch or hanging out after school, going to the movies, and I thought to myself, *These kids have no fucking idea. They are living in a fantasy world, and I'm living in hell.*

After sitting through class hungry all day I would then have to get through a three-hour practice that consisted of two hours of wrestling and one hour of SEAL 6-type conditioning that shouldn't have been legal. After practice, I either had to run a few miles again, or my dad would drive me thirty minutes down to Rider College, where I practiced with the college kids. This was the absolute worst; they didn't hold back, and I threw up sometimes from pure exhaustion. The happiest moment of my day was when my head hit the pillow, even though it meant I'd be starting all over again in a few hours. I felt like I was in the army, preparing for war. This all took place during my sophomore and junior year, and by senior year, I told my coach I was done cutting weight and wrestled at my normal weight even though that meant I'd have the hardest competition. I didn't care. I needed to eat.

On the bright side, I had an incredible group of friends in high school. There were six of us—me, Richard, Jack, Justin, Connor, and Eric—and we were inseparable. We hung out every single day after school and on the weekends. We went to the pool, rode our bikes, and when we all got our driver's licenses, we started driving around and hanging out with girls.

I felt like all of my friends were rich except me. All of them had amazing cars, multiple homes, boats, and jet skis. My friend Justin's dad owned two businesses, and he was always buying new cars or renovating the basement with multiple TVs, an arcade, a movie theater, and a bar that was big enough to be in a restaurant. When wrestling season finished, Justin and I got to work for him at his restoration business for twenty bucks an hour.

Then there was Connor's dad, who made triple what Justin's dad made. They owned an eight-figure flashlight company,

Princeton Tec, and he was a highly successful entrepreneur. The business had been in the family for generations, but when Connor's dad took it over, it grew into the multimillion-dollar corporation it is today. If you've ever bought a headlamp, it was probably made by them. We all worked at Princeton Tec during the summers on the flashlight assembly line, and his dad paid us in cash. They also took us on vacations all the time—we often went to their house on Lake George, where I finally got to rip some jet skis for real. Different toy, but same idea—all those fantasies about ripping snowmobiles that I had in elementary school were finally coming true.

I was experiencing the rich lifestyle and I was loving it. *How could I get the same thing?* I wondered. I wanted a BMW, too. But I was driving my mom's old Acura. I looked at all of these different dads and I thought to myself, *You know, I want to follow one of these paths. They are all living awesome lives.* My dad had created a great life for us, but these guys had all the extra stuff, and it was because they had all taken the extra step and gone down the entrepreneurial route.

My parents weren't giving me money like my friends' parents were, so to keep up with their lifestyle I became a pizza delivery boy in high school. I started grinding early on the days I worked, and I took every single shift they gave me. I worked overtime. I took all the receipts from the other pizza boys who were being lazy and ran out the door to go deliver their pizzas. The gig paid in all cash, and it was awesome. I did anything I could to buy the bottles for the parties.

During my sophomore year, I made a lot of friends on the wrestling team, and that's how I met Sam. He was African American, a year older than me, and he was the coolest. He was probably the most popular guy in his grade, all the girls loved him, and he was an amazing wrestler. Sam and I became really good friends and wrestling partners, and he brought me to all the older kids' parties. I was the only guy in my grade who had this plug, and I started networking with them. This was the year that the partying really started to take over. There was always something fun and exciting going on. I loved going out, staying out past curfew, and partying all night in my friends' basements. We were living the good life. Maybe it wasn't healthy, but it sure as hell was fun.

Since I was so accustomed to all these crazy pool parties, basement parties, and beach house parties in high school, when the time came to pick a college, University of Arizona was one of my top choices. It was considered the mecca of nice weather, hot girls, and partying. Those were my requirements. My dad's rule, on the other hand, was that wherever I went had to be on the *U.S. News & World Report*'s list of the top 100 business schools.

As I searched for colleges and tried to figure out where to go, I watched a ton of "I'm shmacked" videos, which are YouTube videos of all the big party colleges. I found the best ones and then cross-referenced them with the *U.S. News & World Report*'s business school list. It also had to be affordable, so if a school wasn't on the list and affordable, I crossed it off. My final school list included Michigan State, West Virginia, East Carolina University, University of Ohio, Florida State, Arizona State, and University of Arizona.

One day my dad said, "Let's go check out Arizona; I have a business trip out there." Two of my high school friends, Jack and Connor, also wanted to see the University of Arizona, so we took them with us. Once we were in Tucson, toured the campus, and felt the vibe, it didn't take long at all to decide that this was the place for us. In the end, Jack, Connor, and I all ended up going there.

Late in my senior year of high school, my acne became a real problem. I realize now that it came down to my diet, which was horrible, and all of the partying I'd been doing my senior year. Since I didn't cut weight for wrestling anymore my senior year, I was back to eating two bowls of processed sugary cereal every morning and then going out and downing who knows how many beers at night. During the warmer months when I was out in the sun and swimming in the ocean, staying active all the time, my acne calmed down. But once fall and winter rolled around, it came back with a vengeance.

Other than my acne flare-up, my senior year of high school was great. I finished wrestling in the winter and was done forever, which was pure bliss. Late that winter I also found out that I got into University of Arizona, so I basically coasted through the spring. I had a girlfriend, friends, and the lifestyle, and it was one of the best periods of my life. I was so excited to go to what I considered the best school in the world with my two best friends. I had all summer to hang out with my girlfriend, who was from one of the wealthiest families in our town and lived very well. We spent a lot of days at the beach and her beach house that summer.

* * *

August rolled around, and it was time to move to Tucson and start college. I was so excited to embark on a brand new journey in the West Coast. I knew from day one I was just going to get the best grades I could, but I was not going to freak out if I couldn't get all As. I knew I would get by and figure it out.

One of the first challenges I dealt with at college was the fact that I was from the East Coast. It seemed like everyone at U of A was from the West. I was an outcast—my style was different, the way I talked was different—everything was different. I felt like a visitor, especially since I'd just come out of high school with my big ego and fancy friends, where I was one of the coolest guys in school.

My first priority to combat this was getting into a fraternity. I had always envisioned myself being in the best frat on campus, and the biggest one at University of Arizona was Sigma Alpha Epsilon—SAE. I was known for my natural social skills back home, and I knew I was going to get in. The fraternity rush week included two rounds of interviews at the frats, and if they liked you, you would get a callback to the third round. I made it past the first round with ease and after the second callback, I knew I was going to get accepted. But I never got the third callback. There I was, already feeling like an outsider in this whole new world, and I got rejected for the thing that I was best at: being popular. It was a punch in the gut. I felt like my life was over.

I tried for a few other fraternities and finally got into a Jewish frat. I'm not Jewish, but they were opening up to non-Jews and they were known for partying hard, so I joined. I didn't go to the U of A with any intention of becoming Jewish, but I decided to make the best of it. A lot of guys in this fraternity came from successful families and were rolling in money, and I was drawn to that, as usual. I won't get too detailed about pledgeship, but it was crazy. Let's just say it was like wrestling practice without the sport, except this was every single day and I was also simultaneously trying to be a college student. Pledgeship lasted for fourteen weeks and ended with hell week. The final forty-eight hours were spent on top of Mount Lemmon (Tucson's tallest mountain range); it was insane. To give you a hint, I ended up having goldfish for breakfast. And no, not the kids' snack. Actual goldfish.

My freshman year of college would have been all right if it weren't for my face looking like the pepperoni pizzas I used to deliver. My cystic acne went crazy. Once I got into the college lifestyle—eating junk food and cafeteria slop all the time and stressing out because of my classes—it flared up again with a vengeance.

This started a very dark season of my life. I looked around at all of the other kids, and they had no acne. I was jealous and ashamed. *If only I was that guy I would be having so much fun right now*, I thought constantly. The only way to silence these dark thoughts in my head and to feel comfortable in my body was to drink and take Xanax. I even wore sunglasses in the house just because it gave me an extra layer of confidence and I couldn't see the detail of my skin as much when I passed by the mirror.

I couldn't take it anymore. Early in my second semester of freshman year, I made the decision to do whatever it took to fight my acne. After reviewing all the options, I decided I would take the strongest medication of all: Accutane. I would be done in six to eight months, by the end of the first semester of my sophomore year. I would have clear skin. Finally.

Spring break was coming, and I was excited to go back to my girlfriend in New Jersey. I didn't love her, but the feeling of being loved was something I couldn't resist at this point, so I went home planning to see my amazing, loving girlfriend, only to find out she was already dating another guy. Just my luck. That summer, I went to a house party that was kind of a reunion. All my high school friends who had come home from college for the summer were there. It was held at a big house, and the kid's parents weren't home. There were about eighty people there, doing all of the typical things—except for one kid who got extremely intoxicated and decided to pummel my face until I was unconscious. It turns out he had anger issues, and of course, all that anger had to end up on my face. He blindsided me, and the result was catastrophic: he broke my eye socket and twenty-one ligaments. Because of this, today the left side of my face is pretty much made of metal.

After the impact, I woke up on the floor having no idea of what happened. Someone gave me an ice pack and said, "You need to go to the hospital right now." I got to my parents' house at around 1:30 in the morning. My parents were horrified when they opened the door to my broken face. They drove me straight to the emergency room. I still really had no idea what was going on. All I could think was, *What just happened?*

First I was taken to the closest emergency room. After twenty-four hours of initial treatment, they transported me to a surgical hospital for major facial reconstruction. I stayed there for five days. Of course, they put me on all kinds of painkillers and drugs, so I was out of it. When I finally woke up and looked at my face, I didn't recognize myself. It was so swollen and puffy, I looked like a potato. Looking for a positive, I thought to myself, *At least this will be the perfect time to take my Accutane and get it over with since I'll be in bed all day anyway.* I asked my doctor if I could start the acne medication, but she informed me that I couldn't take it for at least six months because my bones had to heal first. Accutane alters bone growth so it's one of the worst medications to take when trying to heal. Great. Now I couldn't even take the one medicine that would cure my acne. Could life get any worse?

Eventually, my face healed. But the battle wasn't over yet; it was Accutane season. A time of isolation, no alcohol, no girls, no sun, and no fun. It was one of the worst times of my life. Especially since I was living in my fraternity house. I couldn't imagine not being able to partake in any of the fun. And then, just when it couldn't get worse, something happened that changed me for the better in a big way.

THREE

IT HAPPENED FOR ME

I T STARTED WITH SPRING BREAK OF SOPHOMORE year. The entire Greek community of U of A was heading down to Cabo San Lucas, and even though an abundance of sunshine and alcohol were the worst things to mix with my acne medicine, I had FOMO and really wanted to go, so I bought the ticket. I went against my better judgment, ignored my gut, and got on the plane. I told my parents I had it all figured out, and promised I was going to be good and wear sunscreen and not drink, but my real thoughts were less innocent. I figured I could drink all week and get away with it. *It's just one week*, I thought.

The minute we left for the trip, I started drinking. We partied all day on the way there, and by the time we got to the airport in Mexico, we were hammered. Deep down, I knew that I had already made a mistake. I felt sick, had an intense headache, and started to worry I'd get kidney or liver failure from mixing so much alcohol with the Accutane.

Since we were all shit-faced by the time we got to Mexico, the last thing we wanted to see was a brutal three-hour customs line that looked like it stretched for a mile. One of my friends who went to another college just happened to be in the front of the line, so we ducked under the dividers and got behind him. We just cut in front of everybody—including all of those families waiting with little kids and older people who just wanted to get to their resort.

I guess the Mexican authorities weren't too fond of this idea, because they took me, the ringleader, and my two buddies into a customs holding room with a bunch of guys holding AK-47s to discuss this bad decision of mine. In the end, we were deported from Mexico. They put me and my two friends back on a flight to the US. Instead of partying on the beach with all my friends in Cabo that week, I had to go back to a practically empty frat house in Tucson and do pretty much nothing with no one over that spring break. My two friends and I were crying. But the surprising thing was that I wasn't crying out of sadness. I was crying out of joy and relief. I knew that this entire scenario had happened for a reason and that I was not meant to go on that trip. I was crying out of gratitude because I knew I had been saved.

There were only three other kids back at the frat house. All of them were holdovers, kids who had nowhere better to go. It was just us, chilling for the next four days until school started back up. These kids smoked weed, but they weren't really into partying like I was. They were more interested in experimenting with psychedelics, listening to music, and playing video games. I guess you could say they were the more artsy kids. So there I was with them hanging out in the basically empty frat, and one night they started talking about LSD. When I told them I'd never tried it, they were like, "Bro, you gotta try it, just once. It'll change your whole perspective."

At that point, I was so lost. But at the same time, I was getting this feeling that someone or something was looking out for me. I had a gut feeling that I should do it, take a risk, and move forward. We took some blankets and a speaker and hiked to the top of Gates Pass, up in the mountains right outside of Tucson. We left around 5:00 p.m., about two and a half hours before dark. We took the tabs at the beginning of our journey up the mountain and by the time we got to the top, we were tripping. The other guys started playing Pink Floyd as the sun was setting. I had no expectations, and that was a big part of why it turned out so well. They told me, "Just let it take you," and so I laid back on the blanket, and soon, the music and the stars started to get crystal clear.

As I saw the constellations in the sky, connected by glowing lines between the stars, I entered a whole new frame of mind. More than anything, I felt loved. We stayed up there for a couple of hours, and it got dark. We were having such an amazing time listening to the music and looking at the stars that we forgot we were on top of a mountain and had to hike down. It got a little scary, especially when we saw a baby bobcat. The other guys were terrified, but at this point, I was so high all I wanted was to take the cat home. Luckily, they didn't let me.

Eventually, we made it down the mountain and got a ride back to the frat house. The music in the car was incredible. I could feel the bass pulsing through my entire body like never before. As soon as we got back, everyone ran up to the bathroom to wash off the mountain dirt. I was afraid to look in the mirror and see my acne, but I did it anyway, and the image that greeted me was completely different than it had been before. For the first time, I could see through my acne, all the way through to the person I was becoming. Suddenly, I felt this profound confidence in myself. I experienced a crazy deep connection with my higher self, and it changed everything for me. I had been so lost and so full of self-hate, but here I was now, able to realign and feel compassion for myself. Sure, I was going through hard times, but I had no reason to hate myself. My inner voice was telling me that life was just getting started, and I was going to be extremely successful. I knew that eventually I was going to be a good-looking guy. I could literally see myself a year in the future, happy and on top of the world. And that's when I realized that no matter how bad it gets, you have to hang in there and never give up.

I pulled away from the mirror smiling and went out to the back of the house, where there was a skateboard leaning up against the basketball hoop. I went over and grabbed it and got on. I hadn't been on a skateboard for a few years, so I thought I'd be a bit rusty, but I started doing tricks just like I had when I was a kid. I got lost in it, practicing my favorite tricks for hours while listening to Pink Floyd's music pour out of the speakers. I felt like a kid again. It was an incredible night that I'll never forget.

That one day turned everything around. I became more grounded. I got grateful for everything, and from that point forward, I stuck out the battle. Even though I had been denied on my first try for the business school, I decided I was going to try again. I said to myself, *I'm going to get that. I'm going all in*. I planned to apply again in the fall of junior year; from there, I'd be able to start up in the business school by second semester.

* * *

At this time, the movie *The Wolf of Wall Street* had just come out. Everyone wanted to be a stockbroker and make a bunch of money in the market. One of my frat brothers' dads worked at an investment brokerage in Manhattan, and he hooked me up with a summer internship. I was pumped. This was going to look great on my résumé and help me get my foot in the door of the banking world. Five days a week for twelve weeks straight, I commuted over an hour from my parents' house in central Jersey to Manhattan on a bus. I worked all day, drinking a ton of coffee in a windowless room for twelve dollars an hour when I could have been doing construction outside for twenty-five dollars an hour with Justin and his dad. That was my whole summer. It was brutal.

One thing I learned from that experience was that I would never become an investment broker. I realized we've all been lied to. There were no fancy beach house parties

34

in the Hamptons or blonde supermodels waiting for those guys at home. Instead, the guys I worked with hustled investments to their clients all week just so they could blow all their money at the steakhouse and the gentlemen's club on Fridays. Banking sucks. By this time I was in the last stages of my acne treatment, and I was focused. Even though I hated the internship, I still made a decent amount of money, hit the gym every day, and got tan at the beach on the weekends. I knew the future was going to be awesome. I was going back to school, and I was going to start living large. This time I was going to be the popular one. My confidence was back and I was ready to go *all in* on every aspect of my life.

Junior year, we moved to the "boat house," an off-campus frat house that was known as the best pool party spot at the University of Arizona. I moved in with the coolest guys in my frat. Since I had been denied from the business school for that semester, I had two options to get the credits I needed to still major in business: pick a minor or just take a couple of Spanish classes to fulfill the language requirement. I decided to take the Spanish classes, but I wanted to take them online so I didn't have to commit to a schedule. I still had money saved up from the internship, so I paid a kid to take both of those classes. All of this put together meant that I didn't have a single class, and I lived at the biggest pool party house on campus.

Instead of going to classes, I spent my days going to the gym and partying. I had the time of my life for that entire semester. At the end of the semester, I got into the business school. Now I was finally having a great time, and on top of that, success. My dreams were starting to come true. I started business school in the spring and pretty much lived the high life for the rest of college: I enjoyed all the partying and the girls, all the while getting good grades and working out a ton.

My dad felt strongly that I should have a minor in college, but I was not hot on the idea of piling on tons of new work, so I found a study abroad program that allowed me to go to Barcelona for eight weeks in the summer following my junior year. Through this, I could get all of my credits for an international business minor *and* I could travel Europe at the same time. I got my dad to agree to the plan and was set to live in Barcelona for two months. I turned twenty-one the day I left for Barcelona. I was with four of my best friends, and we pretty much owned Europe that summer, or at least it felt like we did. We worked for part of the day at our internships for our study abroad credits, and the first chance we got, we grabbed a beer and headed for the beach. We toured all of Spain; we saw San Sebastian, Bilbao, Madrid, Valencia, and Seville…it was beautiful. I fell in love with the architecture of the centuries-old buildings and felt like I was transported back in time a thousand years whenever I roamed the streets. I couldn't believe that my parents had not experienced this side of the world yet.

Even though I was broke, I was making it work. We went to Ibiza for a weekend; took acid on the beach; saw Kygo at Ushuaïa, the most legendary club in Europe; and sailed on yachts. We went to the Lollapalooza music festival in Paris for a weekend and drank wine under the Eiffel Tower. I'd never had that much fun or felt that much freedom before in my life. You may be wondering how my friends and I made all these exotic experiences happen. First of all, we were all very good at networking. Barcelona is full of college abroad programs, and we built up a network of friends, including the promoters of all of the different nightclubs. My friend Nate also had a credit card from his parents that he claimed had no limit. He needed someone to do stuff with, so I tagged along. A large group of girls rolled with us, and it felt like we had this whole mob. Wherever we went, the party followed. I was in heaven.

During the fourth week in Spain, we went to a music festival, Barcelona Beach Fest, and both Nate and I had our phones stolen. Barcelona is notorious for being the pick-pocket capital of the world. Nate called his parents and they bought him a new phone the next day. But I was not getting a new phone; I understood there was no way in hell my parents would do that. So I spent the next four and a half weeks of the trip with no phone but continued to have the best time of my life. Without my phone, I could be totally in the moment. I officially became the "iPad guy." I would bring it wherever we went and blast music on it at all times. It was in Barcelona that I decided I was going to be able to do this kind of thing forever. Toward the end of the trip, my friends kept saying that we should cherish this experience because we would never have one like it again. I nodded and thought, "Speak for yourself." I vowed to figure out how to have this type of experience whenever I wanted it. This wasn't just hanging out with my rich friends in Robbinsville. This was me experiencing Europe and enjoying the most awesome environment in the world. And I wanted more. I had experienced limitlessness, and I decided that it did not have to end.

While everyone else had been working their asses off at internships and coming back to senior year with the most money they'd ever had, I returned to school broke as a joke. My parents had decided that I would have to support myself because of the expense of sending me to Barcelona. They weren't going to help me with any of the trips my friends and I had planned, like Vegas, Coachella, Cabo, or Lake Havasu. I had to find a way to go on these trips, so I needed money fast.

I worked as many hours as I could at my pizza job before going back to school and also worked a few days on a construction project. Still, I only made around $250. That was not going to be enough to fund my big plans. I knew my grandmother had given me some bonds, so I found them in my mom's drawer and took them to the bank. Even though they weren't mature yet and I wouldn't get full value for them, I cashed them in for $750, which left me with about $1,000. That was a lot of money for me at the time, but I still knew it wasn't enough. Once I returned to school, all I could think about was how I was going to multiply this money.

Remember the kid who sold comic books to his mom for four bucks a pop? Well, that kid made a comeback during my senior year of college. My entrepreneurial spirit returned, and I decided I was going to find a way to parlay that $1,000 into much more. I won't go into too much detail, but there were certain party drugs that everyone was doing in college, and so I made an investment, and since I lived in a big party house at U of A, I ran a very successful operation my senior year and financed all the trips I wanted to go on. Yes, I sold drugs. I'm not proud of it, and I am extremely grateful that I never got caught. Thank the Lord for that. My parents never knew, but they were happy because at least I wasn't asking them for money.

Since I had started business school later than everyone else, I had a lot of classwork to catch up on for my major if I wanted to graduate on time. The business school held a job fair in early March, right before Coachella. All the employers in the area came to the school and set up tables, and we walked around and checked them all out. I applied to the payroll processing company ADP, and they set up an interview. I crushed the phone call and then they asked me to come down to their Phoenix office, so I drove down there for an in-person interview. I got the job right away. I was all set to start the job in early August. This meant I had a job locked down with only a couple of months left of school. I could have flunked every class and it wouldn't have mattered. For the last few months of college, I decided to take the partying up a notch. I figured, "I might as well enjoy every last drop before I graduate."

Right after I graduated from college, I went to Europe for a second time. But this trip was nothing like the first one. It was kind of a bummer, actually. During this time, my drinking and partying started to get out of control, and once again, things were about to get dramatic.

FOUR

JUST
GO FOR
IT

BECAUSE WE WERE IN A JEWISH FRATERNITY, the foundation paid for my frat brothers and me to go on a birthright trip to Israel. Even though I wasn't Jewish, they didn't ask questions. Our idea was to get the free flight out there, do the stuff that we were forced to do in Israel, and then fly to Mykonos and party.

We flew to Israel after we graduated and started the party a little early—on the bus in Jerusalem, of all places. The advisors got so fed up with us that they not only kicked us off the bus but off the trip altogether. We had to sign a waiver, and then they left us standing there with our bags in the streets of Jerusalem, practically right where Jesus was born.

We were just three nights into the trip and had already been kicked off. I felt like shit about it deep down. *Why am I such an idiot?* I kept thinking. We had about four nights left before our flight to Greece and not a lot of money between us for accommodations. We pooled our money together and got a shitty room in Tel Aviv for the next few nights, where we all crammed in to sleep on the couches and floor.

Once in Mykonos, we stayed at a hostel and tried to make ends meet. Unlike my experience the summer before, there was no luxury whatsoever. The hostel where we stayed had no air conditioning—in the summer, in Greece. It was so hot that all we could do was drink, especially because we got there in June and none of the big parties started until July, so we didn't have anything else to do. It was sad and depressing. I celebrated my birthday and made sure everyone on Instagram knew how much "fun" I was having, but in reality, I wanted to go home and cry. In a way, I was trying to relive the trip to Barcelona from the year before, which had been the best time of my life. But this trip was nothing like that. It was the complete opposite; it sucked.

One day I was at the ATM getting ready to pull out the rest of my money when the machine sucked up my debit card. I had no way of getting any more money and a week left in Greece before my return flight was scheduled to depart. I was screwed. I had to ask my parents to send me money through Venmo. They sent a little, but mostly I ran tabs with my friends and they spotted me for the remainder of the trip. When the vacation from hell finally ended, we went back to the States, and I got ready to move to Scottsdale and start my new job in early August.

My best friend from the frat, Harrison, also got a job in Scottsdale, and we decided to rent a place together. We weren't sure where in Scottsdale we wanted to live, though, so when we first got there, we decided to Airbnb it for a while. Our plan was to rent in one area for a month, then another area the next month, and just hop around like that until we found an area we liked and wanted to live in.

I'll never forget walking into the second Airbnb we rented. It had probably been built in the '60s, and nothing had been remodeled or refurbished since then. The place was musty and stank of cigarettes, but it was a great deal—just $700 a month each. My room had nothing in it except an old, creaky bed. It had no headboard and was propped up on these little wheels so that it squeaked or moved whenever you sat or laid down on it. Otherwise, it was a very small, completely white room with nothing in it. I didn't want to waste money on a dresser, so I ordered some crates from Amazon and organized my clothes in them. I popped my college desk in there and that was it. A roller bed and a desk. No artwork, no nothing. It was the most depressing room I had ever seen.

I was excited to be in Scottsdale, though. I felt like I was starting a new life, my "real" life. Many of my friends from college had also just moved there, so I assumed it would be amazing. We were all set with jobs that made between $40,000 and $80,000 a year, there were millions of bars and nightclubs and golf courses all around us, and we were going to have a whole lot of fun.

We went to music festivals with girls every chance we had. We went to Rawhide all the time, which was a Western town and event center outside of Phoenix that was always hosting huge festivals. Decadence was a big EDM fest, and there was plenty of Molly going around at that one. I was *all in* on that stuff. Whenever there was a party, we went. Whenever there was a concert, we were there. We took a bunch of drugs, drank a lot, and that was our weekend.

There was one huge problem with all of this. As a sales associate, I made around $38,000 plus commissions. It wasn't that much, and I was blowing it all on partying. I thought I had my shit together, but let's be real, partying my ass off was not what I was supposed to be doing anymore.

Deep down I knew this, and I started enjoying partying less and less because I didn't know what my identity was anymore. I wasn't a student. I wasn't an entrepreneur. I wasn't that good at my job, and I wasn't taking it very seriously, because I had no passion for it. I loved partying and having fun—and I still do—but I was also trying to find my place in the world. Instead of soul searching, I was getting lost in the sauce all the time. I was living for the weekend, living for happy hours. I was caught up in a routine of going out Friday night, partying all day and all night Saturday, with a break to watch football while partying all day on Sunday. Then I'd roll into work again on Monday feeling like death. Not only was it expensive, but it was also totally draining. I had no energy and felt like shit all the time.

At work, I spent my time scrolling through my phone, waiting for any excuse to leave. The first opportunity I saw for a meeting, I was out of there and wouldn't go back to the office for the rest of the day. I was worthless at the gym because I was so hungover. Before long, the partying expanded beyond the weekends—happy hour on Wednesday, hanging out with those random girls we knew who came to town Thursday, and on and on. On nights I didn't have anything to do I scrolled on Tinder and tried to find a girl to hang out with. Every single bar was right next to us, and any night of the week we could roll over and get fucked up.

Slowly but surely, I came to the realization that I was trapped. I wasn't drinking and doing drugs for fun anymore, I was doing it to numb the pain, so I started looking for a way out. My first step was to start doing some personal development. I didn't tell anyone, but I started with the standard personal growth gurus, books, and content—*Think and Grow Rich*, *How to Win Friends and Influence People*, *The 10X Rule*, the Netflix documentary *I Am Not Your Guru*, Tony Robbins YouTube videos, Gary Vee, that kind of stuff. I decided to stick with this for as long as it took and find a way out of the cycle I was in.

Harrison and his girlfriend were inseparable and went everywhere together. They were out a lot, so I often found myself alone in the house. In late November of 2018, around Thanksgiving, I had a stretch of time on my hands. Harrison was gone, and nothing was going on. With all that time and space to myself, I had a lot of time to think. I started to realize that I really, really did not like my job at ADP, and I decided to put my spare time to use and try and make some money online. I bought a course on how to do drop-shipping using the e-commerce platform Shopify. I paid some nineteen-year-old 500 bucks for the course, and I actually sold three products on my own through the store I created. I thought it would be easy and I would get rich quick, but it didn't quite work out that way. In the end, I only made those three sales, and the kid I hired as a mentor ghosted me. I learned quickly that this entrepreneurship journey was not going to be easy, but I had nothing else to lose.

That Airbnb changed my life. One Sunday night, I was lying in my bed hungover after partying all weekend. I stared up at the ceiling in that disgusting room that reeked of cigarettes and knew I had to get out of there. I also thought, "Damn, I would love to get out of debt." At this point, I had $20,000 in student loans, as well as some credit card debt left over from college. That financial burden was weighing on me. I realized I needed to figure out what I wanted to do, and fast.

I thought about going home to stay with my parents for a while. There, I would have no expenses and could pay off the debt and save up some money. Or, I thought, I could get a real place, a one-year lease somewhere, commit to twelve more months in Scottsdale and make something happen by then. It's true that the environment in Scottsdale wasn't great for me, with the partying and the people around me all in dead-end corporate jobs. But I also knew that going home to live with Mom and Dad would be much, much worse. Once you go back to your hometown, all your dreams just die. You go back into living under your parents' roof and your identity reverts to the high school kid you used to be.

I talked Harrison and another friend of ours, Jake, into getting a one-year lease on a place. In December of 2018, we moved into a three-bedroom condo. I had a real room that I could put furniture in and decorate. I shared a big bathroom with Harrison. I was still working the corporate job, and still partying my ass off, but at least I was out of that shithole Airbnb. Now I had the space and freedom to do more and to create more. I decided that over those next twelve months I would figure out my future.

Just a few weeks after the move, one of the newer entrepreneurs I followed on Instagram was hosting a networking event. Without telling my roommates, I packed up my notebook and slid out the door. I was going to be surrounded by millionaires. And thanks to my books, I knew exactly what I was supposed to do: "Fake it till you make it," they said. And I would do exactly that. It was at a kid's mansion in North Scottsdale. His name was Casey Adams, and he was nineteen. At the age of seventeen, Casey started his own podcast after suffering a spinal injury playing football and being told he would never walk again. He got into personal development and interviewed people about it on his podcast and then was picked up by some Scottsdale entrepreneurs and moved into the mansion where he held these networking events. As a result of all this, he built a huge personal brand and became verified on Instagram.

I pulled up to the house to find about one hundred people there. Rolls-Royces and Ferraris were parked in the driveway, and there was a gorgeous pool in the backyard. The people attending were from many different niches, including advertising and e-commerce. By that point, I had already failed my attempt at drop-shipping, so I decided that my profession that day was a content creator. I introduced myself that way to everyone I met: I just walked up and said, "Hi, I'm Colin. I'm a content creator." That networking event inspired me a lot. I met a kid named Anthony Bertoncin there who was hired by Casey to be his full-time content creator. He had dropped everything in his hometown of St. Louis and flown out to live with these guys in Scottsdale and work with them full-time. He was only eighteen years old. I was fascinated with how fast these entrepreneurs were changing their lives.

I had felt from the beginning that the job at ADP was soul-sucking, and early in 2019, I learned that one of my coworkers felt the same way. His name was Brett, and he was always doodling designs for hoodies and shorts and stuff, with the dream of starting a clothing company. He had connections that helped him get the fabric and a factory, and the skills to design the clothing. I had both the desire and the skills to do marketing. We were both craving something creative to do, so we started a clothing line together. We decided to call it Hidden Agenda, because that's what we had: a hidden agenda to become something other than sales guys at ADP. We started our own Instagram page and began producing T-shirts.

Because I wanted to create the best content possible, I bought my first really good camera, a Sony a6300 with a nice lens and a stabilizer. I spent about two and a half grand on it, which was all the money I'd saved up from not going out and drinking as much as I used to. Brett produced the clothing and did the stitching and the graphics, and I was the content guy. I shot promos, edited the videos, all the things I had loved doing when I was a kid skateboarding around Robbinsville. Brett was the star of the videos. I was behind the camera shooting him, and that is when I realized: something inside of me wanted to be the person in front of the camera.

Hidden Agenda was my first business on Instagram. Brett and I made a little money on it, but it didn't last long. We were just testing the waters. My big takeaway was the realization that I didn't want to be just behind the camera shooting and editing. My future was starting to become clear.

But first, I had to learn one more brutal lesson.

Even though I'd slowed down my partying somewhat, we were still going hard on it most weekends. In March of 2019, my friends and I had another one of our epic bender weekends. We had already gone out on Friday night, and on Saturday night we went to Maya, an outdoor club with a massive bar, games, and even a pool. For us, it was just another typical late night out. Around 1:30 or 2:00 in the morning I got separated from my buddies. I was left behind, by myself, and I don't remember anything else. I woke up the next morning in a strange bed with a massive headache and a nasty bump on my head. I looked over and there was a dude laying on the bed next to me who I didn't recognize. I then realized my shirt was ripped and I only had one shoe on. My first thought was, *What the fuck?*

I didn't even wait to look around for my other shoe. I jumped up and ran out of there as fast as I could. The dude looked up at me and said, "Be quiet so you don't wake up the girls on your way out!" My phone was at 5 percent. I called a Lyft and went home. Once I arrived, I went straight to my room and tried to figure out what the hell had just happened. I was trying to piece the puzzle together when my phone rang. It was the cab driver from the night before—the one who had taken me to the guy's place. He told me that my card had been declined, and he was calling to get payment or else he was going to file a police report. That would have been fucked because I was pretty much out of money, but it helped me put the puzzle pieces together because he asked me, "By the way, how are you? You hit your head on the way out of the car. I was telling the dude you were with that you did not look good. Are you okay?"

I asked the driver to tell me more about what had happened the night before and he said that the guy I was with had claimed there was a party back at his house. When I got out of the car, I fell and hit my head on the ground. In all likelihood, I had been roofied. Apparently, I was barely able to communicate, but the guy with me convinced the Lyft driver that I was fine. At the end of the call, I agreed to pay the driver, and I also asked him for the guy's address.

I filled my roommates in on what had happened, we immediately stormed over to the address the driver had given me, and I started smashing on the door. I didn't even know what I was going to say to this guy. But no one answered the door, so we left. Back at home, we all talked about what I should do. Call the police? Press charges? But in the middle of the discussion, I remembered something from one of the books I had been reading: whatever you focus on in life expands. Instead of *reacting* to the situation I took a deep breath and thought about how I could *respond*. I was still alive and I didn't have any aches or pains besides a small bump on my head. I needed to focus on what I could control. I knew I couldn't change the past, but I could definitely change the future.

That day I made the decision to change. That was it. No more bullshit. I was going to change my life. I realized that the obvious way to never put myself in a situation like that again was to stop going out. So from that point on, I was done. I didn't tell any of my friends about it; I just slowly stopped going out. I stopped drinking so much. I kept to myself, and on Friday nights I stayed in my room with my door locked. I forced myself to start looking at myself honestly and to decide what I wanted for myself in life. What did I want to feel like? What did I want to look like? What did I want to do every day? What made me happy?

From the answers to those questions, my morning routine was born. I became focused on building a new identity. I read more books: *The Subtle Art of Not Giving a Fuck* and *You Are a Badass*. I listened to *The GaryVee Audio Experience* every single day. I started waking up at 5:00 a.m. every day and spending that time by myself, working on myself. I bought a gratitude journal and started writing down ten things I was grateful for every day. I decided I needed a big canvas on my wall to dream and plan on, so I went to Goodwill and found a sad, beat-up whiteboard— two of them actually. The previous owner had scribbled all over them with a Sharpie, and the girl at Goodwill said, "Honey, I don't know if you are ever going to get that shit off."

But I bought them both for five dollars total and then used some vinegar to scrub them clean.

I started writing down my plans and goals on the whiteboard. I wrote down how much I would sell at work every month, how long it would take to get my credit card paid off, and a plan for paying off my student loans. After working on my short-term and long-term goals every morning, I went to the gym and worked out and then went to work. I started tracking things in my life instead of just floating around. I cut out everything that represented short-term fulfillment and distraction from the new identity I was trying to build for myself.

If I realized a friend was being overly negative, I distanced myself. I realized that some of the people I was hanging out with the most were complainers. They had a victim mentality. My group of friends mainly consisted of people who just wanted to make their $50,000 to $100,000, spend it partying, and that was it. I loved them to death, but I was ready for a challenge. I was ready for the next step: to set goals, be different, and follow my own path. I was finally going to be true to myself. I was finally going to listen to my inner voice, which was screaming, "This is not the life I want. Make a change!"

After doing this personal growth work for a couple of months, and hitting my quota at work, I started feeling more and more like my job was bullshit. I wasn't enjoying it, and I was barely making ends meet. I felt much more fulfilled by personal development, reading, and the learning I was doing on my own. I started reading a book per week and taking Tai Lopez courses online, and, most important of all, I started going to more and more networking events. I knew I had to go where the people who wanted the same kind of success that I did were going, and that made all the difference.

FIVE

YOUR NETWORK IS YOUR NET WORTH

A S I WAS SEPARATING FROM MY OLD SOCIAL circle more and more, I wanted to be surrounded by successful people constantly, so my newest fascination became networking events. I started going to networking events around Scottsdale at first, and then in the neighboring states, like California and Nevada. I drove all over, attending these events and finding new people to collaborate with. I was still working my job, but I was also experimenting with different ways to make money.

In May of 2019, I went to a networking event that changed my life. At that point, I'd been following this group of kids for six or seven months. They were all in their early twenties, traveling the world, taking private jets, exploring exotic destinations like Bali, Indonesia, and going to all of the amazing places I wanted to go. They ran a webinar all about how to make money with ATM placements, putting them in strip clubs, barbershops, and other all-cash businesses. They taught people how to buy the ATM, fill it with cash, and then draw the service fee. I learned that it only cost six grand to buy an ATM and another $5,000 to fill it. I was trying to figure out some creative financing to pull that together when this group suggested I come to their all-day, in-person networking event in Newport Beach, California. It was being held in their mansion, and I had to pay $2,000 to attend. I didn't have the extra cash at the time, so I threw it on my credit card. There were going to be four speakers: one on ATMs, one on e-commerce, one on sales, and one on credit. I knew I had to go to this, so I hopped in my VW Passat and drove seven hours out to California by myself.

Walking into that networking event, I was more fired up than I'd ever been. I was with all of these like-minded people, many of whom I'd been following online, consuming their content every day. I looked up to them. Now here I was, sitting in a room and talking to them in person. I was laser focused and officially had spent my last dollars for my ticket, so I had to make it worthwhile.

A kid named Justin taught the credit section. I had an immediate gut reaction when he talked about how you can use credit to grow your wealth astronomically. *You mean, I can use other people's money to invest in assets? I can earn passive income with borrowed money? There are cards out there that give you zero percent interest for twelve months? Holy shit!* It blew my mind.

Then there was another guy who talked about e-commerce and automated stores. These stores were $30,000 investments, and they ran on their own. All you needed to do was start an LLC and pay for the products to be drop-shipped with your credit and then you'd make a profit margin on each sale. Some of these stores were producing $5,000 a month passively. By the end of the day, I wanted to do it all. I wanted to get an ATM. I wanted to build my credit. I wanted an Amazon automation store. The problem was I was dead broke. Not to mention the fact that I still had student loans. But the seeds were planted in my head. I was fired up, and I was ready to get this shit done. I needed a way to start making extra money right away.

Before I left, I spoke to Daniel G., who was the high ticket sales speaker at the event. He specialized in selling other people's products and services online. He had a massive sales team and also trained his people on exactly how to sell. I figured this would be a great place to start making money online in my free time. I approached him and told him I'd be reaching out to him on Instagram. He told me later that week that in order to sell for him I had to buy his training course first. It cost $2,000, but he put me on a payment plan because I was so in the hole; $1,000 upfront and $1,000 once I started making money.

As a result of that training course, I started selling other people's products online. I did this on the side, while still working my day job at ADP. I made sales calls for Daniel G. in my car on the way home from work. I made Excel spreadsheets, rolled sales calls all evening, and got my feet wet. It was a great learning experience, but really what I wanted was to sell my own products instead of other people's.

Next, I went to a Grant Cardone real estate event in Phoenix. After he spoke, I was so fired up that I posted my first Instagram story that night. In fact, it was my first time speaking to the camera. At the time, I had about 1,500 followers, which included all my party friends from college. After recording the video three times, and then deleting it each time because I was so afraid, I took a deep breath, stood up, and urged, "Guys. If you are unhappy in your job, if you want to learn new things, I'm telling you, you have to go to networking events. I just got back from Grant Cardone. I learned all about real estate, passive income, and borrowing money to purchase investments. And I absolutely loved it. I'm telling you, you guys have to go."

That was my advice. I let it fly out to my followers on Instagram, and pretty soon people were asking how the event was and saying it sounded awesome. That was my first jump into actually creating and sharing what I was learning.

Another thing I learned around that time was that if you need a loan and you're not in a position to get approved for a business loan, you should apply for a personal debt consolidation loan. The banks don't want to give you a business loan, because then you're going to do business, make money, and pay the loan off. But with a debt consolidation loan, people do home improvements and things like that, things that keep them in debt. And the banks like it when you're in debt. Since I wanted an e-commerce store and I didn't want to wait to save up my own cash, I applied for a debt consolidation loan and was very quickly approved for $20,000. The interest was 11 percent, but I figured it would be well worth it because of the amount of cash flow I'd be generating with my investment. Taking out that loan was one of the scariest things I had done up to that point. I didn't tell anyone about it.

Within a day, the money was in my bank account. It felt so good to see $20,000 in cash in my account. And I found a use for it very quickly. For some time, I'd known about some guys who lived very close to me in Scottsdale and were doing very well with their entrepreneurial ventures, mainly selling Instagram "celebrity giveaways" and "engagement packages," which is how people who want larger audiences can grow their presence—by buying followers. I sent a long DM telling my story to one of the guys who owned this business—let's call him John. I told John how much I hated my job, how I'd just taken out a loan, was ready to invest, and wanted to take action. I told him that I was inspired by what he was doing. He wrote back right away and asked me to hop on FaceTime. I was freaking out. This guy actually answered!

John and I FaceTimed, and then he asked me to swing by the office so he could learn more about me. He was super nice. I drove two minutes to this massive place. It was about 5,000 square feet—all glass, with several Maseratis parked outside. It had a kitchen, a massive boardroom, the whole deal. All of the kids there were my age, ranging from twenty-two to twenty-six. The energy in that place was insane.

I met with John for about an hour, and we discussed what I could do with him and his team. I told him about the debt consolidation loan and that I was thinking about investing it in the Amazon e-commerce automation store I had learned about at the Newport event. John said I should work with him and invest my money in his buddy's e-commerce businesses instead. Along with that, he suggested I invest in my personal brand. "If you want to start making money on your own, you need a personal brand, because your brand is your business."

The light bulb went off for me. Why was I hiding and trying to do e-commerce in a closet when I could be out there building a name for myself and creating a platform to sell things? His plan was for me to invest in an e-commerce store for passive income and then also invest in my social media so I could build my own platform, which was my personal brand. I would build my followers and work under him, and he would teach me everything. The best part of all: I would soon be able to quit my job.

I was totally fired up. I drove back home thinking how awesome it was that I had manifested this. I went to the bank, took out the $20,000 in cash, and bundled it in two $10,000 packs secured with a rubber band. I walked back into John's office, and he introduced me to another guy, who had a little contract for me to sign. I had no lawyer; I didn't think I needed one. I trusted these guys.

I slapped my $10,000 on the table to buy one of his Shopify automation e-commerce stores. *Boom!* I was ready to get automated, to get into some e-commerce. Then I invested another $5,000 into their Instagram growth package as a way to grow my personal brand. I kept the final $5,000 to pay down my credit cards. Paying debt with debt is not good, of course, but I was paying off 20 percent interest debt with 11 percent interest debt, so it was better than nothing.

I posted an Instagram story right away showcasing myself giving my cash to John's partner for my e-commerce store and right away, I started receiving DMs telling me to watch out for John's partner because he was scamming people. I ignored it; there was no way he would ever do that.

On the same day I bought in with John, I met another kid in the office named Pauly Long. Pauly stuck out like a sore thumb. He was from Philly, had tattoos, and was six feet four and bald. I instantly gravitated toward his northeast vibe. The two of us instantly clicked. We became friends, and over the next few days, I started showing him what I was doing with my Instagram, how I was editing my content, and giving him tips on how to do the same thing. He told me that John's partner flew him out to invest in his Shopify store as well. He was only there for a few days. He flew back to Philly, but I got his number before he left, and we kept in contact.

The Instagram growth investment definitely paid off. The way it works is you partner with a celebrity, someone who has millions of followers. The celebrity, usually a movie star or musician, partners with a brand that has a popular product and does a giveaway. They direct their millions of followers to follow everyone the giveaway page is following for a chance to win prizes like designer clothes, a MacBook, or an iPhone. There are usually seventy spots or so sold in the giveaway, and people pay to be someone that the celebrity's followers have to follow to win the prize. Within three days I went from having 1,500 party friends from college following me to having 30,000 followers.

That July, my family took our annual trip to Mexico. John suggested I shoot content while I was down there to build my personal brand. I started taking my content seriously. I'd have my sister take hundreds of photos of me in the infinity pool, on the boat, and on the beach. I would then edit all of my photos with a special app and take my time writing well-thought-out captions. I started to truly understand the importance of branding and the way you carry yourself online. That trip started my true journey of turning my Instagram into a moneymaking machine. Pauly and I kept chatting online about our Instagram growth and e-commerce businesses and the results we were getting. We discussed our dreams of becoming entrepreneurs and traveling the world making money online. Because we were so aligned in what we wanted to accomplish, we became really close.

One day when we were talking on the phone, Pauly told me he was going to do it: he was going to quit his day job as a personal trainer. By that point, I had already decided I wanted to travel the world in 2020, so I told him that I was planning to quit mine at the end of the year as well. That way I would have worked at ADP for a year and a half, and my 401(k) would be 50 percent vested. I was trying to milk my job as much as possible while at the same time learning all of these amazing things about entrepreneurship, credit, and e-commerce. Pauly thought I should quit sooner, but I was dead set on my plan; I was going to do both for as long as I could. The job with ADP was easy money, and it wasn't very challenging, so I still had a lot of energy to do online business development on the side.

Two days after that phone call, there was a knock on my front door. I opened it, and Pauly was standing there. "What's up, motherfucker?" he said. "I'm here. Let's do it." I couldn't believe it. The guy had just quit his job, packed up everything, and driven all the way from Philly to Scottsdale. And now, here he was on my doorstep.

Pauly got himself a room in an Airbnb a few blocks away for $400 a month—some dinky place he shared with some weird girl. Every day after I was done with work he'd say, "Let's go." We went to John's office because we could basically walk in and work for hours on end there, feeding off all that energy. They were also mentoring us on how ATMs and wholesale real estate worked the whole time we were there.

One of the guys at the office, Austin, had a real estate investment business going. He had us knocking on doors in low-income neighborhoods in the middle of August in Phoenix. We'd offer cash for the distressed properties and then the idea was that we would get the contract on it and turn the contract over, making $20,000 or more, all of it profit. That was the idea, except we were never able to close any deals. Instead, we just knocked on a hundred doors a day in the 116-degree Arizona heat, in the shittiest neighborhoods in Phoenix, surrounded by bullet holes and barred-up windows. Door after door after door, and we never got one sale.

We also did the ATM placement that I'd learned about in Newport for these guys as well. Meanwhile, I was selling whatever Instagram growth services I could and splitting my profits with John and his team. My job at ADP was the least important part of my day. I'd show up every morning, go to my one meeting, and then be done. I was just doing the minimum to get by, juggling two lives: ADP and the entrepreneurial life I was dying to have.

I should have realized that eventually someone from work would see what I was doing with John and his team.

But I wasn't really thinking about it; meanwhile, some of my coworkers saw what I was doing on Instagram, and people began to talk.

One day, I got a text from my boss: "Hey Colin, the vice president has found out about your Instagram account. And he finds it concerning," she said. Soon afterward, the vice president called me into his office. As I put on my suit and headed over to the office, I knew it was going to be for the last time. I wasn't ready to quit, but I also knew there would never be a perfect time. I knew he was not going to be happy with me, especially since he had just promoted me to a level where I was selling directly to corporate accountants and earning higher bonuses.

I walked into his office. "What's going on, Colin?" he asked. "When you said you wanted this accountant-centric role, I thought you were going to take it seriously."

"Yes, but I told you when we first met that I had a dream of being an entrepreneur," I said.

"Well, you can't do both," he said. "If you're going to be posting on Instagram during work hours, it has to be about ADP."

I told him I couldn't do that and that I had decided to turn in my laptop and pursue my dream.

"Well, just so you know, Colin," he replied, "I was never going to let you walk out of here with your job anyway."

I got in my car, rolled down the windows, and cruised past the mountains. The sun was setting. I was free! I put on my favorite Kygo song and started screaming for joy. I even filmed a Snapchat story saying "FUCK YOU 9–5!!! WOOOO" that I still have saved today. In that first hour of quitting my job, I knew in my gut that I had done the right thing.

The next day I woke up with more energy than I'd ever had before. I didn't have to report to anyone. I didn't have to go anywhere. I could be with whomever I wanted, whenever I wanted, and work on whatever I wanted, wherever I wanted. Granted, I had no money, and I had a new $20,000 loan to pay off plus $20,000 of student loan debt. I had no idea how I was going to make that happen. But I had my buddy Pauly. He and I had nothing else to do but work, and we were going to grind it out together until we were both making boatloads of money.

We kept at it. We worked in real estate, Instagram growth, ATMs, and e-commerce. At this point in time, there was opportunity in each of these businesses. I was like a kid in a candy store. *Here's a way you can make money. Here's another way you can make money. Here's a way you can sell Instagram growth and make commissions.* It was all sales and commissions, which I had already been doing in my job, so it wasn't that hard to translate that into these other operations.

The work started taking off like crazy, but strangely, the money was not rolling in. The e-commerce store I had bought from John's partner Bill for $10,000 was not panning out. The ads they were running weren't producing any sales on my store, even though I'd been told I'd make two grand a month in sales. Bill and those guys kept promising it was going to happen soon. Then I started hearing stuff from other people, rumors that Bill had been scamming people. The hard truth was that Bill had no idea how to actually run e-commerce stores. I decided to cut my loss fast on the store and instead focus on what I could control, which was selling more services online.

Then I started to realize John, Bill, and their office had been keeping 75 percent of my profits on all of the Instagram services I was selling for them. They had originally promised me a larger share, but I learned the truth: they were not being honest about how much they were making off of all of the Instagram growth packages I was selling for them.

I had to keep at it, though, because I had to keep making money. The Instagram packages were getting more lucrative because John and his associates had figured out a story viewer that would allow people's accounts to view other people's stories. Using an algorithm, they created a bot to watch people's Instagram stories. The bot could watch thousands of stories at once without the person having to actually view them. When that person sees someone watching their stories, they get curious and may write to them and message something like, "Hey, I saw you were watching my story. What's up? How are you?"

This helped me attract tons of attention to my page. I signed up twenty people and made $2,000 in my first week selling the story viewer package working with John, and now I realized I could be making three times the amount if I figured out a way to do this on my own. Now that I had momentum building on Instagram with my own personal brand, I had nothing to lose. I had an audience, and I knew I could succeed by outworking everyone because I was willing to go *all in*. I had no job, and I was in debt up to my eyeballs. I had no choice but to give it my all every single day.

Pauly and I both agreed we needed to distance ourselves from John and his team. We accidentally found the person they were using for the Instagram giveaways and the growth packages through a separate connection. I got in contact with this woman and asked if I could start sending her people and then take a commission from her end. I realized I could make 90 percent margins by selling with her directly. Pauly and I made a quick decision one day when we were leaving the office. We decided we were done with John and Bill and we were never ever going back. We were going to start doing this on our own. We could run all of these businesses without them. At first I was scared to death. But I quickly realized it would be fine; I didn't need them. I understood sales, and I had learned how to do all of these things, thanks in part to their mentorship.

For the next month, we concentrated on selling the crap out of the Instagram growth engagement packages and celebrity giveaways. At night, we would often work and hang out at Aloft in Scottsdale. That's where we met Franny, a bartender who became a friend. She tipped us off to the Marriott Explore program, which offers major discounts—between 50 and 80 percent—to friends and family members of Marriott employees. If the hotel is not busy, the discount can be even higher. The Marriott brand includes hotels like W, The Ritz-Carlton, Aloft, St. Regis, etc.

During that time, I stopped making my monthly payments on my $20,000 loan. I felt like now that I actually had some cash, I wanted to keep it. I'd been screwed over by Bill and John, and not paying the loan seemed like a way to make up for it.

The loan defaulted, and then it went to collections. The bank sold my debt off, and then my credit got dinged and went down below 600. I'd started making money, but now I didn't have any credit. That was not good, because I wanted to travel; I had dreams. And credit is the way to get all that. I started to take some time out of my day every day to learn more about credit.

I realized that credit is like a big, deep rabbit hole, and I should start exploring it more. Did you know that you can get collections and charge-offs removed if the agencies cannot prove that they are yours? In fact, they *have* to remove them by law. I learned how to send dispute letters to all three credit bureaus—TransUnion, Equifax, and Experian. After a couple of tries, and with some help from some other credit experts I was meeting online, one day the $20,000 loan default was removed from my record. My debt was cleared, and my score shot up to the high 700s. The minute I saw that, I turned to Pauly and screamed like a little kid, "Pauly! Holy shit! My credit just went up to 776!" Thank God for unsecured credit, the Fair Credit Reporting Act, and consumer protection laws.

The boost to my credit was all because there was nothing negative on my record anymore. This information was *amazing* to me, and I was documenting it, too, posting content about my successful round of credit repair on Instagram:

"Hey guys, after sending four dispute letters I have a major update. I just got my collection removed off my credit report. I can help you learn how to do the same thing."

Before long, I started to get a bunch of credit-related DMs coming in and realized it had the potential to become another revenue stream.

SIX

CREDIT
IS KEY

O NCE I HAD REPAIRED MY CREDIT, IT WAS game time. Credit was going to be my first key to freedom. From extensive research, I learned that I could access complimentary hotel status, rental car status, airline status, free lounge access, sign-up bonuses equivalent to 100,000 points or more, and TSA PreCheck and Global Entry to skip lines at the airport. I mapped out exactly what cards to get in what order. The first one was Chase Sapphire Reserve. This is one of the best cards because you get three times the points on food and travel. It also came with a 100,000 point sign-up bonus at the time. You also receive 1.5 times more value out of your points when you redeem for travel with the Sapphire Reserve. It is also one of the hardest to get because you have to qualify for a minimum credit limit of $10,000.

The first time I applied, I was denied. So I called the reconsideration line right away, and they denied me for a second time. I didn't give up there—this card was the gateway into all of the other cards I was going to apply for. I needed this one badly. In the credit course I had taken, I'd learned the simple trick of hang up, call again—also known as HACA. So I decided to call back, try to reason with them, and explain to them that I had a high FICO score, perfect payment history, and low utilization on my other Chase cards.

Again, nothing. However, I was relentless. The fourth time, I spoke to a woman who said, "Hmm, there *is* one thing you can do. We can't approve you for the minimum limit of $10,000, but we can let you borrow from your limits on your other Chase cards—the United Explorer and the Freedom Unlimited. We'll reduce those two cards and then be able to give you the $10,000 limit on the Sapphire."

Wow, I thought, *this is working!* The floodgates were opening up, so of course after my approval I applied for more cards.

I wanted to get an American Express card next since Amex is also very focused on travel. I started with the American Express Business Platinum, which is what I recommend everyone do, despite its pricey annual fee. It offers status at hotels—for example, you instantly become a Marriott Gold and Hilton Gold level member. These two statuses will give you access to free room upgrades and more points per stay. Usually, you'd have to stay twenty-five nights to earn this status, but with one credit card, I got it for free. Platinum status could be achieved much more easily at that point because Gold status unlocked the Platinum Challenge, where I only needed to stay eighteen nights in ninety days to achieve Platinum status. Once I achieved Platinum status, I'd have free breakfast, suite upgrades, and lounge access, and this was what I really wanted. I also got the Amex Business Gold, which gave me four times the points on ad spend and food, and the Amex Business Plum, which gave me sixty days to pay my balance, and 1.5 times cash back, which would be perfect for e-commerce if I ever invested in the Amazon automation store I had originally planned to buy.

Finally, the last card I applied for was the Chase Business Ink Unlimited, which gave me zero percent interest for twelve months. So now I had interest-free money to use for investments. The best part was business credit did not report to my FICO, so I could leave a balance for a year and it wouldn't have any negative impact on my score. After all of my credit applications, I was approved for five cards in total. But I wanted a higher limit on my business card to use for investments. I knew $15,000 wasn't going to cut it. The more you can borrow, the more you can invest, and the more you invest, the more you can profit.

I called Chase and told them I thought my business was going to do better than originally expected this year. I said I was projected to make $200,000 over the coming year and asked if it was possible to raise my limit from $15,000. They crunched some numbers and raised my limit to $30,000. I really believed I was going to make $200,000 in the next year, but I didn't have to prove it to Chase. All I had to do was speculate that my income would be going up, and they gave me the credit. Within that one week, I had amassed $85,000 in credit lines, $30,000 of which was at zero percent interest on business credit. Not to mention all of the sign-up bonuses that gave me all the points I would need to book my travel once I set out to explore the world.

Some people think that the more credit you have open, the lower your score, but it's actually the opposite. The more cards you have, the better. The higher the limits you have, the better and the easier it is to get high limits on the next card. The book *Rich Dad, Poor Dad* does a great job of explaining this. Debt is the game. All of the richest people in the world have the most debt tied to their assets. Banks give money to the people who don't need more money.

Once I had repaired my credit and successfully completed what I call "first five card sequence," I was ready to help others do the same, so my next step was to share my knowledge on credit with as many people as humanly possible. I connected with a man named Daryll Drake, who owned a credit repair company and whose content I found to be inspiring. I could just tell from his Instagram posts that Daryll had the best energy. I really wanted to partner with him, so I sent him a DM asking if I could fly out and shoot some content with him, hoping to create a strategic partnership.

"Sure!" he said. "Fly out, I'll teach you a couple of things, and we'll shoot some content. Then we can talk about how we can work together."

Daryll picked me up from LAX in a Bentley the next day, and we drove to Santa Monica. We parked by the beach, where I pulled out my tripod. We filmed some clips of us together, talking about credit repair strategies. I flew back to Arizona the same night so I didn't have to spend money on a hotel. Now I had five one-minute videos with a credit repair expert to incorporate into my brand.

Since we clicked so well, Daryll offered me an affiliate contract with his credit repair company; I would sell the credit repair packages using my social media marketing strategies, keeping $500 and giving him $1,000. His cut was more than I wanted to pay, but I knew it was worth it because he had a very sound system. Daryll was reliable and knew what he was doing. He also had a great support team, which was key. I had learned from my previous partnerships with John and Bill that my strength was in marketing, so that was all I wanted to focus on going forward.

Now I had credit repair locked down, but there were more aspects of credit I wanted to learn about and make money from, like how to apply for each card, how to utilize the points, and how to travel for free.

My problem became my answer. Through my own difficult experiences with credit, I was able to tap into a new industry and create valuable content about what I had learned. Focusing on credit was born from the realization that there were probably hundreds of thousands of other kids like me—people in their early twenties, just out of college, trying to get their lives going and have fun at the same time—whose credit card debt was creeping up while their income was not. Their credit scores were hurting as a result, which led to a downward spiral. What if I started using my knowledge to help those people and make money at the same time?

At this time I started documenting my life on Instagram religiously. I posted videos about my businesses, my workouts at the gym, my morning routine—pretty much everything I was doing to improve my situation. As a result, I built credibility. I told my followers what I'd learned and how I learned it and made myself available to offer them guidance. My thought was, *If people don't know me, why would they pay me?* Deep down I knew that people needed to get to know me in order for me to be successful, and that I needed to let my audience into my life and create a connection with them. I began to direct message every single person who DM'd me. If they hit me up, I helped them. Of course I had some haters, but I knew deep down that they were just jealous and felt guilty that they weren't doing anything to change their negative situations. All publicity is good publicity. I learned from Grant Cardone that haters make you famous.

At this time I was also selling Instagram growth packages and keeping 90 percent of those sales. I alternated days; one day I sold social media growth, and the next day I sold credit repair, back and forth between the two. My posts went something like this: "Hey guys, today I'm doing a special credit repair promotion. Here are some people I've recently helped. Only $1,500 to clean up all of your credit. DM me 'credit repair' and I'll get you to my team right now." All day, I'd collect leads and connect people. I'd get paid. Then the next day, I'd say, "Hey guys, today I'm going to be focusing on growing your Instagram page. We want to grow your personal brand because your brand is your business. You want to be able to promote your product and service. You need credibility. How do you get credibility? Instagram followers. I have a brand new campaign going live on Tuesday for 10,000 followers. All you have to do is pay $850 to enter, and you get 10,000 followers."

When people signed up, I'd pay my promoter and keep the difference. Now I had multiple cash revenue streams coming in with two partners I could actually trust. Of course, I also had my best friend, Pauly, who was not that into credit but was focused solely on the Instagram growth packages. Even though we had slightly different focuses and were not technically partners in anything, we were still working side by side, keeping each other accountable, hitting the gym and the coffee shops and the bar at Aloft together and supporting each other through the journey every day.

The next shift I made would not have blown up nearly as much as it did without another ideal, game-changing partner.

Up to that point, I'd been building the two revenue streams strictly through Instagram stories. I wasn't really posting content. Stories are great for getting people engaged, because they're interactive, but they're also fleeting and don't usually offer a lot of value in terms of information. Stories also disappear after twenty-four hours. Videos, with teaching points and mini-lectures woven into short clips, are better for building a brand over time, and they stay on your page forever.

On October 22, 2019, I posted my first actual video on Instagram. That's when I started directly talking to people and giving them tips on how to master their credit.

My first post was called 5 Beginner Credit Tips:

1. Apply for a credit card ASAP. Do not wait.
2. Put all of your daily spending on your credit card. Put the debit card away.
3. If you are just starting out, have someone in your family add you as an authorized user to their account. Their account should have a perfect payment history and have been open for five years or more. That's how you boost your history when you are just starting out.
4. Open more accounts in order to increase your credit mix. Lenders like to see revolving lines, personal loans, student loans, and real estate loans. So create a wide variety.
5. Keep your balances below 10 percent, or at zero if possible.

That was the beginning of me sitting down with a tripod and giving people the information I knew about credit for free. I started shooting, editing, and posting these one-minute videos, and it didn't take long for me to realize that it took way too much freaking time to do these by myself. Around this time I got a DM from a kid named Shahab who lived in Iran. Shahab sent me a message saying, "Hey, bro, I took this post from you. I downloaded the video and I put subtitles, thumbnails, and edited it for you. I hope you like it. Let me know."

I took a look at what he had done and thought, *This is amazing. He has some serious shit.* Shahab gave value and didn't expect anything from me in return. I thought, *Now this is someone I want to work with.* After a few DMs back and forth I officially hired my first team member: my content editor. Everything after my first two videos on Instagram is all Shahab—the titles, the animation, the logos. He charged me fifty dollars a video, and it was well worth it. I filmed the content and sent it over to him to edit, and he'd make it look slick and add subtitles and then send it back and I'd upload it.

For one month straight I uploaded free valuable videos on how to leverage credit, build income, and travel. Giving free information away online built trust and credibility in my brand. This was an essential step I needed to take before launching my first course.

* * *

My condominium lease would be up in December, and Pauly and I agreed that it was time to get the fuck out of Scottsdale and go on an adventure. Thailand? The Philippines? Bali? We dug in on each one, and Bali stuck out. It had the perfect vibe. It was an entrepreneurial hub. It had nightlife and beautiful villas, and it was cheap. There were many nearby places in Indonesia I could also travel to while I was there. In November of 2019, Pauly and I booked a villa for January 2020 in Bali. It was official; we were going global.

But first, I needed to keep building my brand and finish out the year strong in Scottsdale. Pauly recommended I alternate my Instagram posts between pictures and videos, because it has been proven to be more engaging to audiences. If you look at my profile back then, you'll see a photo of me traveling to some exotic or luxurious place; then a video with tips and information about how to do the same thing yourself; and then a picture, a video, a picture, video, back and forth. In the videos, I say something like "Hey, my name's Colin Yurcisin. I travel the world and educate people about credit. I help people build their credit, earn great incomes, and leverage their lifestyles." That's how I molded my brand into what it is today.

The Instagram saves and shares told the story of how big this could be. If I had 250 or so people saving my videos to watch in the future, and some of them were also sharing it with their friends and family, then I knew I had something. I had not expected this kind of growth so fast, and at first, I was kind of shocked. I thought, *Holy shit, people actually like this stuff.* One of my videos even went viral, with more than 15,000 views. People wanted this information for themselves because they thought it was so valuable. Everyone was wondering about credit, debt, and travel, but no one was actually speaking about it out loud, online, truly giving free value about how to master it like I was. I had information they wanted and needed.

I learned from Gary Vee that the next step was to monetize this information, put it all into a course or a private page, and build a community around it. I loved helping people for free, but if I wanted to make a major impact I needed to start making more money so I could invest back into my businesses and go even bigger.

One day I woke up extra motivated and had a download while I was in the shower. A thought popped into my head that said "Credit Class." I envisioned an online class that anyone could tap into to learn everything they needed to know about credit. I drove over to Schmooze, my favorite coffee shop in Scottsdale, grabbed a nitro cold brew, and got to work. The first thing I did was check Instagram to see if the name "Credit Class" was taken already. It wasn't. I created the account and for the next four hours I compiled all of the information I had learned about credit onto private highlights on the page. It was so simple. My course was just going to be a private Instagram page that you had to pay me to access. Everyone wanted my knowledge on credit, and now I could teach them all my secrets here in Credit Class. By the end of the day I had my completed project, and I began to market it on my personal page.

On Black Friday, I launched my first business: Credit Class. I made a simple story post saying "$250 to join" and the Venmo payments started rolling in. The reason I launched it on Black Friday is because just one year earlier during this time I had bought my first e-commerce course during a Black Friday sale. At that time, I learned that $20 billion was spent online every year on this day. I decided I would give it a try.

My plan ended up working out great. On that day alone, I signed up twenty-six people and made $6,500 in profit! It was that Black Friday energy working its magic. Everyone was looking for deals. And then there was Cyber Monday, too, so the whole long weekend people were just buying, buying, buying, and I was selling, selling, selling.

The best part about it was that there was no overhead for Credit Class. It was pure profit, because it didn't cost a thing to create an Instagram page and use it to market my brand.

After my first successful product launch, I knew that I had just broken through a major barrier. Just three months ago I was working at a corporate job making $3,000 a month, and now I had just made $6,500 profit in one weekend selling my own product.

I realized this was my future: I would continue to acquire knowledge—about social media and brand building, about credit and passive income streams, travel and real estate, everything that goes into creating a lifestyle full of freedom and growth—and then I would teach it to my audience. Everything was coming together, and it felt like a dream come true…almost. There was still something missing, and that was a real badass girl to share my successes with.

SEVEN

THE GIFT
OF BALI

IGHT AFTER BLACK FRIDAY, PAULY AND I
went to Las Vegas. I was so excited after the successful Credit Class launch; I just wanted to celebrate and promote the hell out of it. I'll never
forget the massive seafood tower Pauly and I ordered at
Spago at the Bellagio. I took a story of us toasting each other
while the massive fountain show played right in front of our
table. I knew right then and there that I was officially entering a new lifestyle.

In December, right before our Bali trip, there was one last
networking event I wanted to attend. This would be my first
networking event that I attended as a true business owner.

I was excited to network at a higher level and give value to people I had always looked up to. I figured if I proved to them that I was valuable enough, maybe I'd be able to partner with them in return. The event was hosted by Alex Moeller at the W in Hollywood. Immediately I could tell the difference in my confidence and the way I approached people. Soon enough I had a circle of people standing around me asking me questions regarding credit sequencing, travel, and repair. I was giving out my contact information left and right and was even invited to speak as a guest in someone's upcoming mastermind call. For the first time I felt important, like I had finally found my place and had value to offer to the world.

I took a girl I was seeing at the time with me and rented a Lamborghini for the weekend while we were in Hollywood. Daryll, my credit repair partner, also happened to own an exotic car rental company and hooked us up with the Lambo for a discount. Of course, I shot content of myself driving around Beverly Hills in it, showing everyone the new lifestyle I was hacking into, and how I was truly living my own life by design:

"Hey guys, I'm driving a Lamborghini I just rented from someone in my network in Beverly Hills, and we're staying at the SLS. It usually costs two grand a night to stay there, but guess what? I'm staying there for $300 a night and I'm getting free breakfast in the morning. If you want to learn how to do this, head on over to my Credit Class right now; it's only 500 bucks to join." (I continually raised membership prices until I got to $1,000.)

Right around the same time, I used the profit from selling Credit Class on Black Friday to make another big investment. I purchased a companion pass on American Airlines for $8,000 that would give me an entire year of flying around the world as often as I wanted for no additional money. I did this using a little-known secret: airline employees often sell the companion tickets they are given to use for their own friends and family. Now I could fly standby for free all year. This included first class lay-down seats on international flights at no extra charge. Now I had everything I needed for my global tour.

The morning we departed for Bali, my mom drove Pauly and me to the airport. We flew twelve hours from JFK to Doha on Qatar Airways for the first leg in economy class. It was the most brutal twelve hours of my life. When we landed in Qatar, I decided to drop $1,200 on an upgrade to business class for the nine-hour flight to Bali. I was earning good money at this point, and I knew that if I could film myself flying business class into Bali, it would get everyone fired up. Economy was not the way the CEO of Credit Class should be flying. Remember "fake it till you make it"? That became my philosophy. Pauly thought I was crazy to spend that much money on airline seats, and he stayed back in the main cabin. Meanwhile, I had a flight attendant take my picture on an international business class flight. Just as I had expected, it created a vibe. My followers went nuts with excitement, and I was pumped. It was well worth it to spend one-tenth of all the money in my bank account on that seat. I sipped my champagne and once again knew that my whole world was about to transform.

We landed in Bali at about midnight; it was hot and humid as shit. We took a skinny little taxi from the airport and traveled on all these super narrow roads, where people were driving around on scooters and mopeds. There were entire families with three kids all on one moped. We rolled down the windows and asked the driver to blast some rap. We were fired up.

We got dropped off at the Airbnb and left our stuff there. The villa we rented was a two-bedroom with a pool in the middle, located in the town of Canggu, which is the most popular area in Bali for entrepreneurs and digital nomads. Some guys we'd met online had told us about this beach club that had a huge party going on, so Pauly and I headed down there. This place had a deep house stage, a DJ literally right on the ocean, and thousands of people scattered throughout all of the different bars. It was crazy.

We were out that night until 4:00 a.m., and then we napped for a little while, woke up, and continued to party. We met people who showed us all the fun beach clubs. That first day, we went to a beach club called Alternative Beach that had a rope swing and a diving board, where you could just hang out and jump into the pool all day.

By the end of the day, we were exhausted after partying for almost twenty-four hours, straight after traveling for twenty-four hours to get there. I said to Pauly, "Let's just get some pizza and go to bed." We said our goodbyes to everyone we had met and had been partying with at the day club, and walked out, and then headed to a pizza place nearby. Pauly and I walked in, exhausted and still pretty drunk. I didn't have a care in the world. And then I saw this girl.

She was the most stunning woman I'd ever seen. I was blown away. I walked right up to her and said, "Oh my God. You're the most beautiful girl in the world."

I was so over the moon I didn't even realize her mom was there sitting next to her. I offered to buy them both a drink and she agreed. I walked over to the bar with her and asked her what her name was. "Noemi," she said in the sexiest Spanish accent I've ever heard. I thought to myself, *Holy shit, not only is she insanely beautiful but her name is the same as my biggest crush—Naomi Lapaglia from* The Wolf of Wall

Street. It felt like time stopped and all of the stars aligned. I knew at that moment she was the girl for me. I was so mesmerized that I forgot to order her mom her drink. As you can imagine, this did not leave a great first impression.

I could tell that Noemi knew I was really drunk and tired, but I didn't give up. I asked her what she was doing later, and she told me this was their last night, so they had to get back and get some sleep. They were heading back to Spain, where she was from, in the morning. I asked for her number and she said no to that, too. She offered to give me her Instagram, but that was it. That one Instagram name was all I had. Luckily, it was enough.

I watched her leave Bali on my phone by following her stories on Instagram. I was so bummed she was gone. How could the most beautiful girl I'd ever seen appear and then disappear? Was she gone forever? How could I meet her on my first day and it be her last day? As it turned out, she hit me up soon after she was back home in Spain.

"What do you do?" she asked me. She had been looking at my Instagram and saw that I flew business class on the flight to Bali and had all these awesome travel experiences that I'd been documenting the entire year. I tried to explain Credit Class to her, but she didn't really get it at the time. We started chatting back and forth, and since I didn't think there was much of a chance I'd meet her again, I actually tried to get her to buy Credit Class full price. She said no, because she and her mom had just been traveling for two months. "I'm kind of poor right now. I can't. I'm sorry, but I want to work with you later," she told me. She was interested in my branding and wanted to get more followers herself. And that was kind of it. For the next couple of months, I watched her stories and her TikTok. I didn't know if she was watching me, but I was always looking at her.

* * *

After that twenty-four hour bender in Bali, my party streak ended with a rude awakening. After I finally went to bed after meeting Noemi, I woke up at around four in the morning and started throwing up. I had gotten extremely dehydrated and acquired "Bali Belly," which many people get when they first arrive there because of the bacteria in the water. For the next twenty-four hours I was deathly ill. I could not stop throwing up, to the point where I couldn't even retain a drop of water. Pauly found me in my room at nine in the morning. I couldn't even walk. I told him I needed to go to the hospital, that I was pretty sure I was about to die. He helped me on the back of a moped and drove me to the hospital where I could receive treatment. There they hooked me up to an IV and I continued to puke everywhere. I felt extremely weak. But the IV kicked in after about an hour, thank God. I stopped throwing up and felt ten times better. Until I looked at my bank account.

I had just spent around $500 partying for two days straight, and now this hospitalization was going to cost me a bunch more money. I was getting extremely low on funds. Between that and the Bali Belly, it was a sign from the universe, reminding me that I was there to work. Just those couple of days of overdoing it and then getting sick really threw me off track and messed up my momentum. There was also a twelve-hour time difference between Bali and the US, so we had to wake up super early to start working in order to connect with people before they went to sleep. I knew I needed to get back on a schedule.

I was starting to doubt myself a little because I hadn't made any sales for almost a week, so Pauly and I started waking up at 4:00 a.m. to grind. I was getting worried. My thoughts were filled with negativity, but I fought it off. I reminded myself what Grant Cardone preaches: when things start to get a little slow or scary, you just need to take action. Action is always far better than inaction. Inaction is the birthplace of fear and doubt. Just do something.

I turned to my content and started putting it out relentlessly. I was in Bali! I could do my credit videos on the beach.

So Pauly and I got busy. I filmed Pauly for his content, and he filmed me for mine, and then we sent it off to Shahab just like we'd been doing all along in Scottsdale. IGTVs, stories, posts, all of it. Within a week, the money started rolling in again. I had doubled my price for Credit Class—from $500 to $1,000. It was a big jump, so at first sales were slow, because some people were wondering why they suddenly had to pay $1,000 when the week before it had been half of that. But I stuck with it. I knew in my gut that what I was offering was worth it, and I couldn't retract what I'd put out there. Sure enough, after a week and a half, the dry spell was over.

In Bali, Pauly and I also joined a gym—the best one in town—called The Body Factory. It was expensive, $300 a month, which was crazy for us. But this place was sick; it included a spa package, cold plunges, a pool, hot tub, and sauna. As you'd expect, a ton of networking happened there. All the most popular people in Bali, all the digital nomads, were there. We would usually work out in the afternoons, because that's when everyone in the US was sleeping. After the gym, we ate and chilled for a while and then went back to work again, because our nighttime was morning in the US and people were back to work.

Back in those days, I wasn't tracking my sleep like I do now. I didn't give a shit. If I woke up, I worked. We ate out for every meal because an incredible plate of food in Bali cost around five dollars. All in all, we were probably spending thirty dollars a day, living like kings. And we were working in the cafes—Nude Cafe and Milu by Nook were our favorites— so we were making money at the same time we were eating. We even sparked deals with a lot of the Bali cafes and restaurants. They would give us free meals just to post their food in our stories. I felt like I had become a real Bali influencer.

Early in the trip, a mutual friend of mine from college realized his buddies Jack and Ted were in Bali at the same time that Pauly and I were, and so he connected us with them via Instagram of course. They had just rented three properties up in the mountains of Bali in Ubud. Jack and Ted swung down to where we were staying, and we all grabbed lunch. Pauly and I walked in and sat down with them and could feel right away that these guys were extremely nice. They had just sold another business, a spring break tour and travel company. With the money they'd made from those ventures, they were buying up Airbnbs. We were impressed. We hadn't dug into Airbnb yet and we were eager to learn more.

They invited us up to see the places they managed, and we agreed. We went up to see their houses, and we all got along really well. I got them to sign up for Credit Class, with a 50 percent discount for letting us stay at their house.

I dove into more and more credit hacks with Jack and Ted, and they were really into it. They loved my business and what I was doing. We clicked so well that we decided to take a trip together. We went to Gili Trawangan, one of the three Gili islands, a beautiful spot famous for surfing, snorkeling, and magic mushrooms. They only allow bicycles on the island, so it was very unique. It was a huge party island. We rented an Airbnb there and hung out and partied for three days.

I tried to surf one day while we were on Gili Island. I paddled out and attempted to stand up and catch a wave several times, but mostly I just fell and paddled a lot. The waves tossed me around like a twig—I had zero experience. I looked up, and Jack and Ted were surfing these huge waves. They were killing it. I was like, *What the hell?* It turns out that they had both been professional snowboarders in college.

Then we went to this crazy place: Mad Monkey Gili Trawangan. It had a sick infinity pool, and we played beach volleyball and watched the sunset and then ran into the ocean, all while tripping on the famous Gili mushrooms. To this day, it was one of the most beautiful sunsets I've ever seen. Gili Island was about a forty-five-minute boat ride from Bali, and from the beach we could see this big-ass volcano on Bali. It had smoke coming out of the top of it, and in the background was the sunset and the clouds, and the sky was lit up with shades of pink, orange, and red. It was incredible. We splashed around and hung out with everyone at the bar and had a great time.

That night we hit the bars and clubs, and I really got to know more about Jack and Ted and all of their business and travel experience. I realized I'd never had any friends who were true entrepreneurs, but Jack and Ted were for real. They were a few years older than me and had already built a business, sold it, and moved on to their second business. In their off time they surfed, snowboarded, and went skydiving, which was something I'd always wanted to do. And the best part was we connected well on credit. They explained to me how their father had built their credit scores up since the day they turned eighteen. I was excited to show them how they could tap into business credit and use it for their Airbnb business.

Pauly was more into the mindset coaching that he was developing; he wasn't really interested in credit like I was. But these guys were different. They were doing exactly what I wanted to be doing. I just knew I wanted to do business and travel with them. They inspired me, and I was excited to keep meeting more entrepreneurs now that I was one myself. A couple of days after the Gili Islands trip, Pauly and I took a day trip to Nusa Penida, also known as Bali's "black magic island" due to the legends of evil spirits who ruled there and the penal colony that existed there hundreds of years ago. T-Rex Beach is one of the most iconic Instagram spots in Bali, if not the most. Influencers flock there to shoot content against the background of its fantastic scenery. We knew our trip would not be complete without a picture in front of it.

To get to T-Rex Beach, we had to grapple our way straight down one of the slick, dinosaur-shaped rocks. The ladders were all broken, and you could see some of the people who were trying to get to the beach falling off the side of the rock all the way down to the sand. Once I got down to this amazing beach, I filmed an inspirational video and some ads for my businesses, taking full advantage of the location. This was the grand finale, the icing on the cake of a truly amazing trip to Bali.

Before leaving Bali, I told Pauly that we needed to stay in some hotels so I could promote my brand more effectively since a big part of my business is staying in hotels for free or at a discount. I talk about hacks for getting great deals at hotels all the time, and I needed to step into that here and be the magnet. Pauly didn't want to pay for a hotel room, but I told him, "Just come with me; I'll get the room." We rented mopeds and went on a four-day excursion to the Nusa Dua gardens area and stayed at all the different Marriotts there, shooting content the whole time. I walked around each suite, showing everyone the space and explaining how I got the room on Marriott points. Then I walked through all the steps to make it happen.

Even though we were still paying for our Airbnb and I ended up spending an extra thousand dollars on hotels, I got so much great content that it really paid off with a lot of new business coming in.

Once that was done, I realized I needed to keep the travel going. I was getting complacent in Bali. I had done everything I wanted to do this time around, and it was time to move on, time to get on an airplane again. I was ready to pick up the pace, ready for my first really big travel hack.

I wanted someplace I could shoot a lot of content. Someplace viral. Why not Dubai?

I was going to take this trip by myself, since Pauly was loving Bali so much he wanted to stay. Neither one of us thought much of it; there were no hard feelings. We were sure we would hook up again very soon.

I was going to do a hop to Dubai, maybe hit Europe, travel around, and then come back. We'd booked a one-way ticket from New York; our future was wide open. Going back to the States was the last thing on my mind—I mean, why would I? I was having the time of my life. I was making enough income to survive while exploring the world, and I could have gone on like that for three or four more years. Just going wherever the universe took me. So I said, "Pauly, I'll be back, bro. I'll see you soon."

And that was the last I saw of him for a long, long time.

THE JOURNEY IS EVERYTHING

Working at ADP in my cubicle (ready to quit)

When I realized bringing a sweatshirt to London in the winter wasn't the best idea

The whiteboard that changed my life

The private jet on which we escaped the Mexico hurricane with our new friends

The networking event in California where I first learned about credit

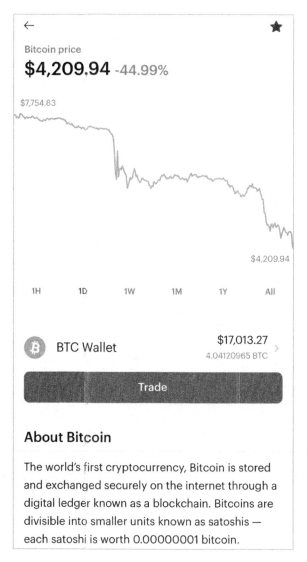

The first 4 bitcoins I purchased at $4,200

Feeling on top of the world on the famous T-Rex cliff at Kelingking Beach, Bali

The breathwork retreat I hosted in Tulum

The Airbnb I rented in Miami that would later become my building

The $1,100 business-class upgrade I paid for on the way to Bali (so worth it)

Thanksgiving on the yacht with the fam in Cabo

Snorkeling in Hawaii

Skydiving in Dubai after pulling an all-nighter

Sailing in Croatia with Noemi, summer 2020

Riding camels in Israel before getting kicked off the trip

Renting my first Lambo in Beverly Hills

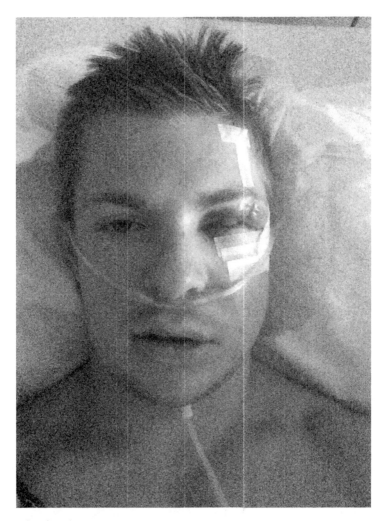

After facial surgery

Paris trip, summer 2017, craziest summer of my life

Parasailing with my new girlfriend

Tulum villa we rented on the beach when we launched Credit Class

Noemi's first time seeing Hollywood

Noemi, her friend Carmen, and me in Tulum

Noemi and me on a yacht in Cancun

Noemi and me in love in Cancun

Mom raising me

The first property I purchased in Philadelphia

My first private Jet

My first Emirates business-class flight to Dubai from Bali

Mud baths in the Dead Sea

Me, Jack, and Ted at our Airbnb in Arizona

Me and Dad on vacation in Mexico

Me and my best friend, Sam (from wrestling), at his prom

Maldives

Little League baseball with "the flow"

Me and Jack hiking a mountain in Arizona

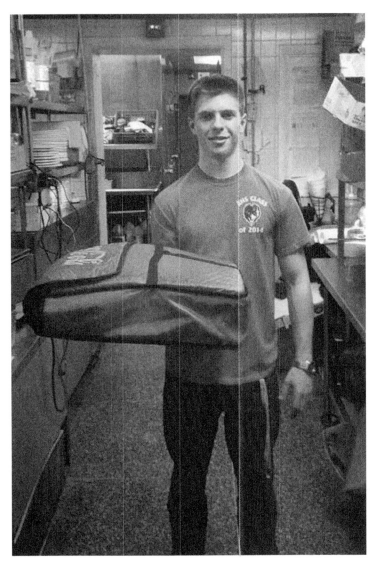

Hustling at the pizza shop, about age twenty

Helping Mom do the dishes

Flying home from Dubai with Noemi

Festival days when I was working at ADP

Dubai

DUBAI SHIT

Clothing company photo shoot

Attempting to be a content creator

At our Hawaii house with Jack and Ted, showing off my cards

In the hospital after I was beat up at the party

Tulum

Noemi and I living in Tulum

EIGHT

JUMP
INTO FEAR

FLEW TO DUBAI IN STYLE. SINCE I HAD 130,000
points saved up, I was able to fly business class. Amex
wanted over 900,000 points for the flight on the
Membership Rewards portal, but since Emirates is an
airline partner you could transfer 130,000 points to Emirates
Skyward Miles and get it for eight times cheaper! Emirates
is considered the best airline in the world, and it has an
insane business class, with special touches like a glass of
Dom Perignon in your hand after you board. Once again, I
was marketing, showing myself at the next level. I sat next
to a woman named Sylvie who owned a wine company in
Paris, and I posted a picture of us with the caption "Meeting

new people like Sylvie, traveling the world, and experiencing what a $4,000 seat on an airplane feels like LIGHTS A FIRE INSIDE OF ME"!"

The overnight flight took nine hours. I had booked a 9:00 a.m. skydiving outing the next morning and was so excited I couldn't sleep. After landing in Dubai, I went straight over to Skydive Dubai, strapped in, and jumped out of a plane. In the air I looked down and saw the massive Palm Jumeirah below, which is the man-made island in the ocean that looks like a palm tree. After a minute of free fall screaming in joy at the top of my lungs, my instructor pulled the chute, and we sailed down peacefully to the landing. On the way down I thought to myself just how incredible life had become since I went *all in* on my dreams. I used to look at pictures of Dubai on Instagram and dream about going, and here I was skydiving over the most legendary spot in the world.

Next, I headed over to the Dubai Mall, which is the biggest mall in the world. I looked at all the jewelry stores, checking out Rolex watches and Cartier bracelets. I only had about $11,000 in my bank account, but I really wanted a white gold Cartier bracelet in particular. I had always wanted something sleek and high-end to raise my frequency and enhance my style. It was a dream bracelet, and how sick would it be if I bought my first piece in Dubai? It was out of my comfort zone, but I put it on my credit card. I used it as a hack, too, because there was no sales tax, so I saved $800 on that. I had to move money around to put it on my Freedom Unlimited card so I could get the maximum points—1.5 per dollar spent. I even had to call the credit card company to get the purchase approved, because I'd never spent that much on a credit card before. Even when the salesman handed it to me, I could hardly believe it. I'd just bought a $7,000 bracelet. *This is insane*, I thought.

That purchase left me with just $4,000 cash in my bank account. If my parents had known what I had just done back then, with how little money I had and the debt I still owed, they would've thought I lost my mind. But I was taking a risk, and I firmly believed (or was trying to believe) what Napoleon Hill says: you have to take risks and get out of your comfort zone to affirm to the universe that the life of your dreams belongs to you. You have to act like the person you wish to become, and the Colin I wanted to become bought nice things whenever he pleased. So I wore my bracelet as if it was something that came naturally to me. Keeping this abundant vibration going, I checked into the JW Marriott Marquis, which is the second tallest hotel in the world. Thanks to my recently achieved Marriott Bonvoy Platinum status, I was upgraded to a huge suite with amazing views. I had a drink to celebrate my achievements at Vault, the bar on the seventy-second floor of the JW Marriott, which offered an insane view, looking out at the ocean and the entire city. The vibe was amazing. I could feel all of the energy both within and around me. I knew I was breaking barriers into my new lifestyle.

I didn't want the day to finish, so after the drink, I headed to the top of the Burj Khalifa, the tallest building in the world, and had a meditative moment overlooking the city. I paid $300 for the rooftop tour and was served tea, champagne, and hors d'oeuvres as I gazed out at the lights of the city.

I had spent a total of $8,000 in just twenty-four hours, but what I did in the next few moments would make a couple of thousand dollars back very soon.

I sat down with my camera and shared the experience with my audience:

"You guys. You can do anything. Four months ago I was working at a corporate job. I was in debt. Now I have money, I have a business. I just went skydiving today. I bought this dream bracelet. And now I'm on top of the tallest building in the world, Burj Khalifa. This shit can happen so fast. If you're feeling complacent or stuck, or that your growth is being stunted, just go. Change your environment, and jump out of your comfort zone. Get to someplace new and see what you can do. It can change your energy and the energy around you. I just did it. I left and I went to the craziest place on earth and just did a bunch of crazy shit. Instead of going to work tomorrow, try taking a day off and driving to who knows where. A national park or the beach, and just have a day where you break the chain of the hamster wheel. Take action. Do something that scares you. It's going to make you feel better and help you become that person you are born to be. Take the leap and do it. Take the chance on yourself. **Go all in.**"

The next day, I moved to a hotel on the marina side of town. The Westin Marina was on the beach, and I got another insane suite upgrade. I mainly just worked, producing a ton of content. Then I went out to dinner at Pier Seven, which someone had recommended to me as a great place to meet people. This place had seven different restaurants, one on each floor. I hit the sushi place and met two German girls who were sitting near me. After we ate, they invited me to get a drink at the top of the building. There was a DJ, and we just hung out, talking and getting to know each other. What a nice way to finish my seventy-two hours in Dubai, huh? I had an early flight to London the morning after. I had planned to stay there for a week, but when I got there, it was brutally cold and kind of miserable, especially in comparison to the warm weather I had just experienced in Bali and Dubai. I'm not sure what I was thinking, going to London in February; all I had to keep myself warm was a hoodie. It was ridiculous. This thing called COVID-19 was starting to get bad in China, and it was spreading to Europe from there. I had started hearing little hints of it when I was in London. Flights were being canceled, and it occurred to me that maybe I ought to get closer to home before it turned into a pandemic. It was still February at this point, but it was starting to become a real possibility. I realized I needed to do the sensible thing and get back to the US.

Wherever I went, I was always walking the talk, always documenting. I flew back to the States from London on a first-class American Airlines flight, using the companion pass I had recently purchased. I documented this, explaining to my Credit Class members how I had bought the airline employees' companion pass and could now fly anywhere I wanted to go for a whole year.

The first-class cabin on that American flight from London to JFK had lie-flat seats, which I was excited about. I figured I would eat good food for eight hours, drink some wine and hang out, while advertising and working. Beats sitting at a desk job, right? I was traveling the world, making money. Going back to the US hadn't been my plan, but

I would just make the most of it. I could just travel around in America for a while and get to the rest of the world once COVID was over.

I landed at JFK and went back to New Jersey to see my parents for a bit. I shared with them all of my crazy stories from the last month and a half of traveling. Then it was time to venture off to Las Vegas and Grant Cardone's 10X Growth Con, scheduled for February 25.

This event was a huge turning point. I had a lot of intentions going into it, and I thought about what I wanted to manifest and my objectives. First, I wanted to find more strategic partnerships. Since I hadn't done any speaking engagements yet, I was hoping to find some opwwportunities for those as well. And in general, I was excited to meet more people who could open doors for me.

A couple of entrepreneurs from Houston who had been following me asked me to come speak at their networking event the following weekend, so I landed my first speaking engagement out of the Vegas trip, just as I'd hoped. I also met a future credit repair partner there, too, a guy named Sean. I met a team of course-builders who I eventually hired to help with my new website. And then there was another guy who was into e-commerce and wanted to help me get started with an e-commerce store. I went *all in* and bought my first

Amazon store shortly afterward, using my zero percent business card with the $30,000 limit.

Also in Vegas, I met a woman, let's call her Lanie, who was
a successful entrepreneur from London. Lanie was running
a seven-figure business when I met her, even though she
was only twenty-three. She had already been listed in *Forbes*
magazine. I was very impressed, and even more excited
when I realized she was into me. We hung out and hooked
up. Being single and having a solid personal brand went very
well together. Having money also made getting girls a lot easier. I could buy them dinner and drinks without having to
look at prices, and if I really liked them I could fly them out
to me or take them on a trip somewhere nice. She messaged
me before the event and suggested we meet at the Cosmo to
get to know each other. From that point on, we talked and
hung out often. At the end of my time in Las Vegas, she asked
if I wanted to go to Mexico with her in a couple of weeks, and
I said, sure, why not? Usually I was the one used to paying
for everything, but this chick had more money than me and
would get everything for free by doing YouTube collabora-
tions. It was awesome.

My first speaking gig in Houston went great, and the hosts
Ali and Shawn also invited me onto their podcast, which
allowed me to reach even more people. It was my first big

podcast in an official recording studio, and it felt like I was a rapper on tour stopping by all the radio stations in each city I visited. In twenty-four hours I had spoken at my first private networking event and recorded an hour-long podcast episode. It was fun, and I was getting shit done with no time to waste before jetting off to a new spot.

After Houston, I flew to Hawaii to meet up with a girl named Gabby I'd met at the Hollywood networking event a year earlier. We'd kept up on Instagram since meeting that night, and she seemed like a fun girl to explore with, so I invited her on the trip with me. It was still February, so the skies were still open. This was going to be my first time back to Hawaii since my parents took me on vacation when I was fourteen. I was so excited to do it on my own dime and have no rules to follow. On the flight over I had the idea to film a montage video for Instagram of my life over the past few months. I needed to start posting lifestyle video content of me traveling to motivate my followers. Hawaii was the perfect spot because it had beautiful hikes, hundreds of beaches, snorkeling and scuba diving, and cliff jumps. My number one goal of this trip was to put together the most badass montage.

When I landed in Maui, I hired a local editor and videographer. I found him on Instagram by making a single story post and tagging my location. His name was Kea, and he doubled as our tour guide, taking us all over the island in his Jeep. We went to all of the coolest spots, like the road to Hana and Wailea Beach, and then we stayed up editing the video until three in the morning. It was my first real promotional video that had a story behind it. I even narrated my voice in the background to make it emotional. I dropped it on Instagram, and within a few days it became my highest performing video I'd ever posted in terms of engagement. I realized the credit class was selling more than ever before. This planted the seed for me. Content equals currency.

From Hawaii, I flew directly to Cancun and went to Tulum with Lanie. It was now early March of 2020. I fell in love with Tulum's beauty right away. Lanie and I stayed for two weeks, working on our businesses and collaborating. Toward the end of that time, the pandemic was announced. On March 12, Bitcoin dropped drastically from its $8,000 pre-pandemic price to $4,000 in a matter of hours. There was a liquidity crisis in the US economy when the pandemic hit, and everyone pulled out of their investments. But the smartest people saw an opportunity to buy low.

I had not invested in anything at the time besides myself, but I had about thirty grand saved in my bank account from all the business I'd been doing. I thought to myself, *Holy fuck, this is how billionaires are made—in times of distress and chaos.* It was a crazy, eye-opening experience for me.

Sitting at dinner, Lanie and I looked at each other and said, "We need to buy assets now." Since I already had Coinbase open on my phone and didn't know shit about stocks, I clicked "Buy Bitcoin" and purchased five bitcoins for just $25,000. I went *all in.* Over the next few days Lanie and I took our time to research Bitcoin. We watched YouTubes, listened to podcasts, and read some books on it. But I also had my eyes on the stock market, and it continued to go lower. A few days later I indecisively sold all of my Bitcoin and went back to cash. I decided I wasn't going to invest in anything until I had a better understanding of it.

Soon after the pandemic was announced, I decided I should get back to Hawaii. It made me nervous to be in Mexico during a pandemic, without all the infrastructure of the US. What if I got sick or injured? Would my insurance even cover me? I wasn't sure. Besides, in my mind, Hawaii was the shit. I figured if I had to be locked down somewhere, it might as well be Hawaii. I could be locked down there forever. I knew I had to act fast because once lockdowns went nationwide, I probably wouldn't be able to get into Hawaii. Once again, I hacked my way there, flying first class in a lie-flat seat on American Airlines, and shot a video of myself eating an ice cream sundae on the plane while the entire world was breaking down in chaos. I said, "Man, am I grateful for the decisions I've made over the past six months. I could not have timed this better."

In Hawaii, I booked a nice two-bedroom villa at the Westin for two weeks, for just one hundred dollars per night. The villa is usually $2,000 per night, but I got a deal through the Marriott Employee program, and since we were in the beginning of a pandemic, no one was traveling.

I struck the deal of a lifetime with this place. I had my own kitchen, pool, and ocean views. I was living like a king and all I had with me was a (fake) small Gucci duffle bag and my laptop. All I wore during this period were cheap H & M black T-shirts, bathing suits, and shorts. I had two pairs of shoes, one pair of jeans, and a black hoodie. There was no need for any fancy shit. All of my money went into my business and travel—food, transportation, and hotels. I was addicted to the feeling of ultimate freedom, and nothing else mattered.

I spent late March and early April hunkered down solo in my Hawaiian villa. I felt like I was living out a version of *I Am Legend*: the whole world was going to shit, and I was locked down in my compound planning ways to build my empire. I worked intense fourteen-hour days and took breaks to eat, work out, and jump in the ocean. I filmed an entire course for

Credit Class, devoured a PhD's worth of information about investing into different asset classes, and marketed my services. Around this time, I came to the conclusion that Bitcoin was the best asset class to invest my money into. I decided that I would pass on traditional markets and instead save all of my money in Bitcoin.

To me it just made so much sense. I learned that the US Federal Reserve had to keep printing unlimited money to keep the world afloat but eventually every fiat currency fails. The United States would be no different. I wanted to preserve my wealth in a scarce asset class that could not be controlled by any single party. Bitcoin was exactly that, with a fixed supply of 21 million. So I began buying Bitcoin at around $7,000 with a very long time horizon. At first, I was completely fine being alone and just working, but toward the end of that fourteen-day period, I got really lonely. I wanted to be with entrepreneur friends who inspired me. What was the fun being in this amazing, beautiful place if there was no one to share it with?

The pandemic had taken over, and Marriotts were closing down all over the world indefinitely. They let me know that they were kicking me out as soon as my reservation was over. It was a little creepy, because by the end I was the last person left in that hotel. Luckily, they couldn't cancel my reservation.

They literally had to stay open just for me. But it was kind of depressing. All the staff wore masks, the restaurants shut down, and it was just bad vibes. All the other hotels around there were shutting down as well.

I was in a predicament. I either needed to go back to the mainland or find a house somewhere in Hawaii. I absolutely did not want to be locked down in New Jersey in late winter, with my family and unable to travel. I decided to reach out to Jack and Ted and see what they were up to. I learned that their Airbnbs in Bali were all shut down because of the pandemic, and that Bali had shut its borders to outsiders. Jack and Ted had gotten out of there and gone back to Washington State where their parents lived. The whole tourism industry was a mess. I asked them what they were planning for the next couple of months and suggested we all get a house in Hawaii. I had already talked to a friend from college whose grandmother had a place on the other side of her house on Oahu. "Let's do it!" Jack and Ted said. So my friend arranged for us to take his grandmother's place for a month. Jack, Ted, and I split the cost, each paying about $1,200 for the month.

I booked a flight from Maui to Oahu on a small propeller plane. It was one of the sickest rides of my life, and I will never forget it. On the way, this little tiny plane passed over Molokai, which has massive volcanic rocks like in Jurassic

Park, and waterfalls that must have been thousands of feet high. The flight was only thirty minutes, and I spent the entire time looking out my window. It was the coolest shit I'd ever seen. Once again I felt like I was in a movie.

The house we rented was on a little beach called Punalu'u, near the North Shore but not quite all the way there. It was basically a deserted little town with a gas station, a deli, and ten homes on a nice secluded beach. Although my friends' grandmother lived on the property and her family came to visit, we didn't see them much since they were in a separate house. Every day, we would get up, do our morning routine, work out on the beach, do some work, go swim and surf, and just enjoy the Hawaiian vibes. Even though we were entering a pandemic, it was probably one of the most peaceful environments I've ever experienced.

The first week, we just hung out. We surfed and caught up, and I ended up teaching them a little more about credit. I looked at how I could help them build their brands more. They already had sick personal brands with incredible travel content, but they hadn't pushed any online business through it yet. One thing led to another, and soon I decided, hey, why not just invite them into my business?

First, I shot content of them applying for and getting their business credit cards. I went through the whole sequence with them, as if I was teaching it online, but I did it with them in person. I documented them getting approved for $55,000 at zero percent interest. Their excitement was clear—they loved the business and wanted to work with me. I suggested they put together a pitch on what they would be bringing to the table to Credit Class, and they went *all in* on it. Their presentation was impressive, and lasted an hour. By the end of it, I was convinced it was the right thing to do, and so, in April of 2020, we joined forces.

NINE

FIND
THE
WIN-WIN

THAT TIME ON OAHU WAS BEAUTIFUL. WE WOKE
up every day at the crack of dawn and worked for
twelve hours minimum. We didn't drink any alcohol for the entire month we were there, although we
did buy a hookah and smoked it every day at sunset. We also
took shrooms one morning and watched the sunrise from
the beach. It was beautiful.

At this point, I was earning good money between Credit
Class and my new Amazon store. I had another $30,000
in cash saved up, so I decided to deal with my remaining

debt. I had gotten it all down from the $50,000 ($20,000 personal loan, $20,000 student loans, and $10,000 in credit card balances) I owed six months earlier to about $20,000. Now I was ready to pay it all off, including my student loans. Psychologically, it was a huge deal to finally become debt free. It was a massive weight lifted off my shoulders. I now had multiple streams of income, a new network of entrepreneur friends, a decent chunk of money in Bitcoin, and zero debt.

Pauly reached out to us from Bali while we were on Oahu and asked if he could come join us. We had mixed feelings about this. Jack, Ted, and I were all working together on Credit Class, and we were focused on scaling that, so Pauly didn't quite fit into the picture. Especially since the business that he had been developing, which was called Mindset, was completely different from what we were doing. It was focused mainly on personal growth and manifestation. However, I'd just had an amazing six month journey with Pauly, and without him I wouldn't be where I was. So we called him up and told him to join us.

Pauly traveled all the way to Hawaii, but it turns out that my friend's grandmother was not comfortable with someone coming from Bali and staying in her house during COVID. We didn't even think to ask her first. We broke the news to Pauly that he couldn't stay, and he was shocked. I felt horrible.

I just had my buddy fly halfway around the world to meet us, and we couldn't even stay together. Pauly was upset, and since he already was there he ended up renting an Airbnb in Oahu that was a few hours away from us.

Toward the end of the month in Oahu, Jack and Ted and I decided we wanted to be where there was more stuff going on. It was a little too quiet for us on this perfect private beach, and we craved more civilization and stimulation. We were working out with only these downed palm tree logs for weights, and we all needed to get back to the gym. We needed more space to do our work, and not just on the beach. We needed an office to work on Credit Class. So we decided on Arizona. We'd have good weather, access to all the technologies, and everything else we needed to build out this company with a better course, a better website, and better content. I also had my VW Passat there sitting at a friend's house, so we'd have a car, too.

We were torn on what to do about Pauly. I didn't know how to break the news to him that we wanted to leave the island so soon after he had gotten there. So without saying anything, we just booked our flights and left. I felt like shit about it, but I didn't know how to tell him we didn't have a place for him in Credit Class.

We found an insanely gorgeous 5,000-square-foot mansion in Gold Canyon, Arizona, that we could rent for a month on Airbnb. It had a pool, was in the desert but up on the mountains, and had an amazing view of the sunsets.

Our goal was to settle our business terms and contracts and then build out a truly professional online credit course for Credit Class. The original terms I had verbally agreed to while we were still in Hawaii were that Jack and Ted would each get 30 percent and I would keep 40 percent. But on the plane ride over to Arizona, I watched *The Social Network*, and during the scene where Mark Zuckerberg screwed his partner out of the company, I had an epiphany. I realized it wouldn't be smart for me to give away more than half of my company. I had created this myself and needed to keep control of it. As soon as we settled into the place in Gold Canyon, I sat down with Jack and Ted.

"Guys, I want to work with you," I said, "but I'm not giving up more than 50 percent of my business." They agreed, and we decided to take a different approach. After that, Jack and Ted flew out three of their other friends they had been telling me about. Jay and Quira were course-builders and had just made their own course on travel, which was doing really well, and Bobby was a videographer, so he set up all the video equipment and ran that. Now there were six of us in that house working on building my company. We then had to sit down one more time and factor in Quira's, Jay's, and Bobby's percentages. Since there were now five new people involved, we came to the conclusion that for the first two months we should do a trial run before anyone got any ownership of the company. We decided that each person would go on a vesting schedule. Each month, as long as you performed in your duties, you would vest more of an ownership percentage in Credit Class until you got to your final ownership percentage.

I had paid the guys from Houston, Ali and Shawn, to put together my existing course, which was okay, but we'd built it on a laptop and an iPhone camera, and it wasn't as slick as it needed to be. The goal now was to have a professional team and create a professional course. We dialed in for a month and conquered the course, the advertising material, e-books, video sales letters, all of it. We purchased professional lighting from Amazon, as well as a teleprompter, and turned the living room into a studio. We filmed for multiple days and perfected the course material. We finished it off with a killer video sales letter, and then Jay and Quira put everything together on Kajabi. Going forward all we had to do was market our new product, and that would generate the whole revenue stream for Credit Class.

It was hard for me to go from working by myself to working with a team of five people. I just wanted to have awesome friends to travel with, so I figured bringing them in as partners was the best option. The one thing that didn't sit well with me was the need for serious contracts at the early stage my business was in. Just a few months earlier I had created the Instagram page for Credit Class, and now here I was signing contracts with "vesting schedules." I didn't even understand what half the verbiage meant, nor did I care. All I wanted to do was travel and make money with cool people, so if contracts were part of that, I guessed I had to go along with it.

Another thing that was evolving at this time was my e-commerce partnership with a guy I had invested with around the time I was at the Grant Cardone event. This was a separate business, but it was tied to Credit Class because I referred people from my course to my e-commerce partner. They used their high-limit zero percent business credit cards to invest into their e-commerce automation store to create passive income. I earned a $5,000 commission for anyone I referred who purchased a store. The money started to pile up quickly. Once the new and highly improved course was finished, we decided we would all head to Tulum, since that part of Mexico was one of the few places in the world that had not shut down during the pandemic. We had originally dreamed about traveling through Europe all summer, but that was shut down as well. We rented a villa on the beach in Tulum that was appropriately called Casa Playa. It was seven bedrooms with a pool and affordable because we landed an influencer discount and it was the off-season. We had been working so hard to get everything set up with the course and the finish line was in our sights! I prepared another marketing plan that mimicked what I did for the original Credit Class sale on Black Friday in 2019. When we got to Mexico we stayed at the JW Marriott in Cancun for the first couple of nights before driving down to Tulum and then launched the course from there. Over the next two weeks we generated $80,000 in profit altogether. This was just shy of our $100,000 goal, but it was still a major success.

Once we got down to Tulum, Jack and Ted invited the girls they were seeing, and I wanted to invite a girl, too. This girl had to be special. I had told Jack and Ted about Noemi when I was with them in Bali, and they convinced me to take a shot at her. *Fuck it*, I thought. I had been following Noemi's TikTok religiously since I'd first met her, watching her daily dance videos, so I knew she was in lockdown in Spain. I sent her a message on Instagram: "Have you ever been to Tulum? I just launched my company, and we're going to be shooting a ton of content. It's going to be a lot of fun. You should come! I'll fly you out." She thought I was kidding at first, but then she realized I was dead serious. To her, it sounded like the perfect escape plan from Spain's draconian lockdown. But she had a condition. She would have to bring her best friend with her. Now I would have to pay for two tickets. But I really, really wanted to see her, so she convinced me pretty easily.

But there was someone else we had to convince. Because of the lockdown, Noemi had gone back to her mom's house, and when she brought it up to her, she was not feeling it. She said something like, "You mean the drunk asshole that didn't buy me a drink in Bali?"

Her mother was so adamant that Noemi was not going to come to Mexico to see me that she hid Noemi's passport. Noemi told me all this, and I said, "Let me talk to your mom on FaceTime. I'll show her I'm a good guy."

I filled the boys in on the situation, and the next morning we drove to town and set up our laptops at a coffee shop with the best Wi-Fi. We were all wearing button-down shirts and looked our best. It was time to convince Noemi's mom that we were gentlemen and would take good care of her daughter.

By the end of the call, Noemi's mom was not only okay with her coming out to Mexico but even said, "Noemi if you don't go, I'm going!" So I flew Noemi and her friend Carmen out the next day. According to Noemi, she told Carmen on their flight to Cancun that she wasn't really into me; she just thought it would be a cool opportunity to travel and meet successful entrepreneurs. She even practiced some "help me" signs with her friend in case I tried something.

I drove to the airport to get them and was so excited to see her. It was a dream come true. Somewhere between the plane and my car, she must have changed her mind about me because, as I later found out, on the drive down to Tulum she mouthed, "He's mine, don't touch him!" to Carmen in the rearview mirror while I was driving.

I wanted to be a perfect gentleman on the first night, not creepy. I didn't want her to think I'd invited her to Mexico just to hook up. I was proper and extremely nice. But we were having an amazing time already. The chemistry was on that very first night. We sat next to each other at dinner and shared laughs and drinks. Her broken English was the sexiest thing ever. I'll never forget how beautiful she looked when she laughed and how crystal blue her eyes were. When we got back to the villa that night we were both brushing our teeth in the bathroom between our separate bedrooms. We were flirting and making each other laugh, and I kept thinking to myself, *Do I make the move now?*

Then Noemi came over to me and told me that the water jug in her room was empty and that she would love it if I could refill it. I said, "Sure," and I ran back up to my room and shut the door to think for a second. Instead of getting her the water, I ended up locking my door and going to bed. I wanted to keep the promise I had made to myself that I wouldn't make a move on the first night, and I knew I wouldn't be able to hold myself back if I brought that water to her bedroom.

The next day we barely spoke at breakfast, and then I went to the gym as usual. I could feel that the chemistry wasn't there anymore. She was ignoring me, and I could tell I had made her confused. When I got back, the boys broke out some tequila and started playing music, and we all jumped in the pool. After a shot or two, Noemi swam up to me with a fierce look on her face and said in a very stern voice, "What's up with you Americans? You're too slow! I almost died of thirst waiting for the water last night. Do you want me or not?"

I couldn't believe it. The girl I had been obsessed with for the past six months was asking me if I wanted to be with her. I laughed and told her about my first-night-non-negotiable-no -hitting-on-her-rule. She couldn't believe it, and I couldn't hold it back anymore; I kissed her. Shortly after that, we went up to my room, and after a few hours we were in love. Seriously, it was that quick.

From then on, we spent every minute together. We slowly drifted away from the rest of the group. The business went out the window. I was too busy going to my favorite restaurants, exploring cenotes, eating tacos, and drinking tequila with Noemi. She and I even stayed two nights at a boutique hotel (of course I got an influencer deal on the room) instead of being at the house with everyone else. The rest of my team made the decision to leave Mexico earlier than planned since we were not around as much. They could see that I had checked out for a while, and all business dealings were off for the time being.

Noemi and Carmen were supposed to fly home after a week, but I decided the only one getting on that plane was Carmen. Noemi was staying. She agreed, and after we dropped Carmen off at the airport, I suggested we stay in Cancun for a couple of nights since we were already there.

We stayed at the JW Marriott and had the best time. Noemi had never seen such crystal blue clear water or stayed in so much luxury before. We got couples massages, went parasailing, and rented a yacht at sunset. We were completely high on being in love. I even had my record day in business and generated over $30,000 in profit through e-commerce referrals. We then went back to Tulum and hung out with my first ever credit repair partner, Daryll and his crew for a week. Noemi clicked immediately with his crew, and we all hung out together. Everything seemed like a blur. We were falling in love and having the time of our lives in Mexico.

The money was rolling in from all the work I had put in the past few months, but I knew I had to get back to the grind, so Noemi and I agreed that she would go back to Spain for a little while and I would get back to work.

In August, Noemi and I met back up in Croatia and went on a sailing trip for a week, which sounded a lot better than it turned out to be. Sailing Croatia has always been on my bucket list, and it was also one of the only places in Europe that stayed open during the pandemic. But we booked a sailboat that we shared with three other couples, and that was the problem. Cramming into a small sailboat with three other random couples for an entire week got a little claustrophobic. The captain took us all through the islands, which were unlike anything I've ever seen before—just super quiet and beautiful. Noemi and I were still falling in love, and everything was still like a dream.

Crazily enough, while we were out at sea in Croatia, I met my now-COO, Gavin. There I was, out in the middle of the Adriatic Sea, on a sailboat with my new girlfriend, and I went online looking for a company I could hire to run ads for Credit Class. I had a Zoom meeting with an ad agency I found on Instagram, and this guy Gavin was on the call. After the meeting, he reached out to me, told me how much he enjoyed my content, and said he wanted to partner with me. So we set up a meeting to discuss it, and the next thing I knew, I had myself an operations manager.

There was only one more thing to fix. The whole time I was in Croatia, I was also realizing that I had made a mistake by partnering with a team instead of hiring employees. Deep down I wanted to run my business myself—with a team of course, but as an individual owner, not within a partnership. When I got back from Croatia, I had my attorney draw up a dissolution contract for the arrangement I had made with Jack and Ted and the team. This was one of the most stressful things I've ever gone through. It was so overwhelming. I was filled with anxiety and some grief, too, because I felt like I was losing my friends in the process. It's so rare to find people that you can live with for months on end, travel with, and do business with. It was very hard to say goodbye to that.

In the end, we figured out an agreement between us that worked for everyone. They signed off on it, and I paid them all out what they were owed for their work. Everyone ended up in a good place, but for a while, they wouldn't talk to me. I thought to myself, *Maybe this is karma for leaving Pauly on Oahu.*

Shortly after the trip to Croatia, Noemi met my family when we celebrated my dad's birthday in Playa del Carmen, Mexico. At that point I was focusing mostly on e-commerce.

I had my Amazon store and was sharing the results all the time on Instagram, advertising: "Hey, I have limited spots available, message me if you're interested. My store is doing $40,000 a month in sales right now!"

I was still working with my first e-commerce company partner but was basically just a broker. He paid me a commission to bring him business. In spite of the loss I felt over the dissolution, it still felt really good to be keeping 100 percent of the revenue coming in from Credit Class. I was much happier being my own boss, free to move how I wanted without having to constantly come to an agreement with a team.

After Mexico, Noemi went back to Spain, and I rented a month-to-month apartment in Philadelphia and just worked. There were zero distractions there, but it was close enough to my mom and dad that I could visit. It was during this time that I dove into real estate. At this time I offered a high-ticket six-week mentorship program as an upsell to Credit Class members; one of the week's main focuses was real estate. So it only made sense that I bought a property.

I called up my buddy Francis Magnubat, one of the top real estate agents in Philly. I had met him at a Vemma backyard meetup seven years earlier. Remember the multilevel marketing company Vemma that ended up being a pyramid scheme? Well, it turns out that everyone I met that day in that backyard in New Jersey ended up becoming extremely successful. Francis and I had followed each other on Instagram since then, and he was constantly educating others about real estate and talked a lot about growing his real estate portfolio in Philly. Now that I had money, I reached out and told him I was ready for my first house.

The cool thing about having Francis in my corner was that he had all of the connections in Philly. He knew the right neighborhoods to buy in, he had relationships with the builders to get the house before it went on the market, and he could get me a house that had a ten-year tax abatement, which meant I only had to pay tax on the land for the first ten years, which saved me a ton of money in the long term. Plus interest rates were at an all-time low of 2.25 percent for FHA loans. I had to get my dad to cosign the loan with me due to only having one year of tax returns.

I bought my first house—a nice three-story, four-bedroom in a quiet part of an industrial neighborhood, with a rooftop view of the city. I only had to put down around $20,000. The best part was that I found three tenants to move in as roommates just by posting a story on Instagram. "Looking for three hungry entrepreneurs in Philly who want to live in my new house. I'll only be there a few months out of the year. DM me 'PHILLY' if you want to move in." Within three days,

I had three tenants sign a year-long lease, which Francis also drafted for me. It felt effortless.

The place wouldn't be ready until November, so I continued renting my apartment in Philly and grinding. I was staying at a place called AKA, a super luxurious month-to-month apartment. We were still in the pandemic, everyone was masked, and no restaurants were open. That was okay because I went straight into monk mode. I locked myself down. I did a juice cleanse and a three-day fast to kick it off. I cut out all coffee and all stimulants. I ordered premade meals and just worked fourteen hours a day.

Around this time, I made a move to break off from my first e-commerce partner. The results he was getting my clients were average, and there seemed to be a lot of problems. Also I had already advanced to the highest commission tier, and he wouldn't agree to pay me more for the value I was bringing. Instead of just getting commissions, I wanted to own the entire business. I knew I needed someone to handle all of the operations, because I sure as hell didn't know how to do that shit.

So I went on the hunt for that next person. As I was doing research, I got a DM from a guy named Steven. "Hey," he said, "I have an amazing opportunity for you. I know the people that everyone's using out in Bangladesh. It's a company that can basically get these stores started up for you and you only have to pay them a few grand and then you charge your clients whatever you want. They will manage all of the operations, and you just focus on bringing in clients."

I talked to the owner of this operation, George. He was based in Malaysia, and his operation was a white label service based in Bangladesh. I had a strange feeling that this was not going to last long, but I figured it couldn't hurt to try it out. At the very least I would learn something. E-commerce was hot, and if I wanted to capitalize on the opportunity I needed to have my own company.

Around this time, I formed a new LLC and asked Francis to connect me with his business attorney so I could get a client-facing contract drafted right away. On August 20, I launched my first solo e-commerce business. I told my original e-commerce partner that I was switching over to another company, resigned our contract, and thanked him for the opportunity. He seemed perfectly fine with it.

TEN

FORM
STRATEGIC
PARTNERSHIPS

GOT MY FIRST E-COMMERCE CLIENT UNDER MY NEW business on August 25 and made $35,000 from that one sale. Instead of $7,500 commissions, now I was generating $20,000 or more in profit per client plus making a 15 percent profit split on the back end. In the first month I had seven more clients sign on and generated $140,000 in profit. I was in awe. I couldn't believe the amount of money hitting my bank account. Some days I would watch two to three incoming wires roll into my account, and I'd just sit back and think to myself, *What the fuck is going on?* Everything seemed to be going great, and then I met Mike.

Mike had reached out to me via Instagram the same week I started my own e-commerce company. He told me that he had his own e-commerce company and a warehouse in New Jersey and he'd been following my stories and found them inspiring. He also said he'd love to work with me and asked if we could hop on a call. At first I brushed it off, because I was enjoying so much success on my own, but something in my gut told me to call him anyway.

On the call, Mike told me he owned a massive Amazon FBA operation, which stands for "Fulfilled by Amazon." There's no drop-shipping involved. All the orders are fulfilled through Amazon; you just source the products, package them up at your warehouse, and then send them off to Amazon, and it takes care of everything else. He said he would be willing to create my own FBA store free of charge in exchange for referrals. He also filled me in on a new platform, Walmart, that his company was automating for clients and doing extremely well with. I was excited. The only problem was that I was already committed to building my own company with George overseas.

I wished I'd heard from Mike just a week earlier, but I had a feeling that partnering with him was the right thing to do.

When we talked on the phone I was struck by all of our similarities. He was about my age, from New Jersey, and hungry. He owned his entire vertical, had built in-house software, and had in-house employees. My gut was screaming that this was the right guy.

So now I had to cut the cord with George and my newly found operation. I immediately stopped onboarding new clients to my newly found business and called George to explain the changes I was making. It took me the rest of the year, but eventually I got all of the clients who were willing to move with me over to Mike's operation to move, and I parted ways with George.

Even though I'd only been experiencing large-scale success for a few months, I had wanted to get my dad a store as a gift, so instead of accepting Mike's FBA store for myself, I gave it to my father. The store did great; my dad made $15,000 profit in the first few months. After these results, I was excited and I knew I had made the right decision partnering with Mike.

At that point, I was stuck on Amazon since it was all I knew, but Mike kept sending me the results he was getting for his current clients on Walmart. These stores were doing three times better than the Amazon stores and had not run into any suspensions yet. Not many people had gotten into it yet; there were only about 15,000 sellers, whereas Amazon had 7 million sellers. Once again I knew I had to make a major change on the spot. I trusted Mike, so I said, "Screw it, let's blow this thing up!" My first big task was to convince my old clients who were going to switch over to Mike's operation from the Bangladesh guys to make the move from Amazon stores to Walmart stores. It was a juggling act for a while, but eventually it all settled out. My clients trusted me, and the results of the stores spoke for themselves. I began the switchover to Walmart stores, and sure enough, it caught fire right away. We went from zero clients to two hundred clients in just a year and a half, and the business grew from zero to eight figures in total revenue. This is when the real money started coming in—multiple six figures per month profit became my new norm.

In early September, I booked a flight to Cancun and met up with Noemi again. We headed down to Tulum to stay at Nomade, the top-rated boutique hotel in Tulum and one of the only places in the world you can justify spending $1,000 a night to sleep in a tent with air conditioning. We hoped to stay there for a while. At that time of the year, the fall and winter, the water in Tulum is crystal clear, and the weather is perfect, except for the occasional hurricane. The breeze blew lightly most of the time, and we were surrounded by jungle on one side and the Atlantic Ocean on the other. The place was pretty deserted, probably due to the pandemic, and I was able to get a great deal on our room.

After we settled in, I went up to the front desk and said, "Hey, we absolutely love your place. We would like to stay here for a long time. What's the best you can do for us?"

She went to get the manager. I repeated my question, asking if we could stay for a month. "Is there anything you can do for me?" I asked.

The manager was stunned. "We've never had anyone ask for that before. I'll see what I can do."

They marked the room down 40 percent, so I got it for $325 a night. I ended up paying just under ten grand for the month to stay in a rustic but luxurious air-conditioned tent on the beach. I didn't put on a shirt for the entire stay; I just chilled, did yoga, made YouTube videos, did podcasts, and promoted my businesses.

One day, Noemi and I decided to smoke bufo aka DMT (the venom of a poisonous toad) together. The Mayans figured out centuries ago that if you smoke it, you can have a spiritual out-of-body experience, lose your ego, and transcend into infinite time and space. Everyone has their own version of the experience, but in my opinion DMT is the most next-level thing you can do in your life. I had been studying up on people I admired like Joe Rogan, Will Smith, and Aubrey Marcus, and all of them spoke about how much of an impact DMT had on their lives. I knew I was ready for it. I had so much momentum going and a whole new vision for my life. I was ready to break another barrier.

This ritual is preceded by a strict regimen. You have to go a minimum of one week eating a vegan diet and not drinking any alcohol. This might sound easy, but if you know me, you know how much I love my steak, and being surrounded by margaritas all day was not the best atmosphere for cutting out cocktails. We pushed through that, but the day we were supposed to do the ritual, a huge storm rolled in, so we postponed it to the next day. Noemi thought this was a sign that we shouldn't do it, but I had already made up my mind.

The next day, it was game time. We had to fast all morning, and then we arrived at the teepee, where we met our shaman. To be honest, he didn't really make us feel at home. He simply asked who wanted to go first, and Noemi volunteered. I'm guessing this is because she wasn't sure it was a good idea, and she wanted to get it over with before she chickened out.

She went into the teepee with the shaman while I waited outside. I was feeling nervous and I kept having to go to the bathroom for some reason. And then the scariest thing happened. Noemi started screaming at the top of her lungs from inside the tent. This went on for at least five whole minutes, and I looked around frantically, wondering if I should go in and save her. A worker walked by and came up to me and with a completely relaxed attitude told me that this was completely normal. *Okay*, I thought. *That does not make me feel any better.*

Noemi's whole experience lasted about fifteen minutes, and then she went out the back of the teepee so that I wouldn't see her before my trip.

Then it was my turn. *Holy shit*, I thought. I went into the tent, sat down, and right after the shaman began his explanation of the ritual, I interrupted him. I had to rush to the bathroom again. I almost shit myself. When I came back he helped me calm down by having me focus on my breathing. I guess you can't smoke the pipe if you're hyperventilating. When I was ready, he handed me the pipe and told me to inhale it for ten long seconds. I felt my throat grow hot and scratchy in reaction to the toad poison.

The experience was frightening; actually, it was the scariest shit of my life. Right after I started inhaling the pipe, I completely forgot where I was and what I was doing. I felt like I had died. *Did I just overdose? Get hit by a car? Was this it?* My last thoughts were about my family and how I had so much unfinished business on this earth. I was rolling around violently on the floor as chaos erupted in my thoughts, and then it shifted. The shaman began to rub my belly to calm me down, and I felt a huge rush of love and energy in my stomach. I focused whatever consciousness I had left on that loving energy, and all of a sudden everything was warm and inviting. I felt the energy spread throughout my entire existence, and all of a sudden, I transcended. All of the thoughts floating around in my head were gone, and my ego dissolved completely.

I let go of Colin Yurcisin and turned into something that was merged with the divine. It was like I had gone to heaven. Imagine the feeling of your best orgasm and multiply that by one thousand. That's how it felt; it was pure love. I've never felt more connected to that kind of energy in my life. I felt surrounded by many energies, and it was as if I'd known them for many lifetimes. I could hear them telling me (without speaking) that they were so proud of me and I could feel their endless love and support.

Finally, I started to come back into the room. I opened my eyes and thought, *Oh my God. I'm back. I'm alive. I have feet. I'm lying in this tent. In Tulum. This freaking shaman is rubbing my belly.* It was the craziest, most exciting experience ever, and it was truly life changing.

Noemi's experience wasn't as amazing. It was pretty horrible, to be honest, and I'm glad she decided not to talk to me after she left the tent, because if she had, I might not have entered it. She wasn't able to fully let go but she worked through that, and a month later, through her own deep meditation practices, she had a very similar experience of completely letting go, trusting, and being held by universal energy that I had. You have to be ready for it to happen.

Tulum became our own little piece of paradise. We loved the people, the hotel we stayed at, the restaurants, the warm blue ocean, and the free yoga classes. We never wanted to leave. One morning we woke up and went to breakfast as usual, and as I was digging into my favorite acai bowl, we learned that a hurricane was hurtling toward Tulum. All of the buildings around us were getting boarded up, and the streets were filled with cars and people fleeing.

We were told by hotel staff that we needed to leave right away. *What?* We had paid for a whole month and only been there for a week and a half. Everything just came to a screeching halt.

Noemi and I went into reaction mode. We had to get out of there, but we didn't know quite what to do. I called a friend in Miami and asked him what he knew about a possible hurricane hitting Tulum. He told me it was a category four. "Look out your window. It's a beautiful day right now, right? That's what happens right before the storm hits. You're going to be underwater within twenty-four hours. You have to get the fuck out of there."

I was thinking, *This will be fine. I'll just get an Airbnb somewhere in town. We'll come back to the hotel once it's open again. In a couple of days this will all be fine.* But my friend sounded so serious. He said we needed to fly home that night. I checked on flights, and there was nothing. They were all full or canceled, and now I was really starting to freak out. I grew panicked about my businesses, too—I had all this momentum, and everything was going great. What if we actually got rolled over by a category four hurricane in Tulum? There was no infrastructure here. There would be no power. The internet would go down. I began to search for solutions. I had to get home so that I could keep the momentum going. As a last resort, I went on a private jet broker's page on Instagram and hit him up. I asked him what was the best he could do for a flight from Cancun to Miami that afternoon. He said it would cost $19,000.

I was horrified at first; that was half of all my cash in my accounts. Everything else was in Bitcoin, and there was no way in hell I was selling any of that. But something told me it was all going to work out. I knew I should just do it. I would get content on the private jet. Worst case scenario, at least I'd make it home safe with Noemi. I thought abundantly and said, "All right. Let's do it—charge my Amex."

Noemi and I got in a taxi and had the driver get us to the airport as fast as possible. It was already four o'clock and the plane was supposed to leave at six. I could not believe this was happening. I had been having the best time ever and now in the blink of an eye I had to hustle back to the States and pay twenty grand to get there.

We pulled up to the private jet airport, and it was chaos— people were running around everywhere. There were very few private jets available, and everyone wanted one. The woman behind the check-in counter told me we were very lucky that we were using a Mexican jet company. Our plane was based in Mexico, so we were good. They had already closed the tarmac to outsiders; no jets from other countries could get in.

I was relieved that our plane was there and we could get the fuck out. But then I realized there were people who needed to get out of Mexico, and we had four extra seats on our jet. Maybe I could hack this situation, and help some people out at the same time, by selling the extra seats on our plane. I went up to a few people and offered them seats for $5,000 each. They were so grateful, and I had four passengers within a couple of minutes. In the end, I flew home to Miami on a private jet for free. In fact, I profited $1,000, and since I had put the tickets on my Amex, I earned 35,000 points.

After realizing that I had just pulled off the impossible, I went and bought a bottle of tequila from the airport duty-free shop. Everything was going to be great! To top it off, the people we rode home with were awesome. We became friends with some of them and met up with them months later when we went back to Tulum. Nomade ended up giving me a hotel credit, which was fine because I knew I'd be coming back soon anyway.

Noemi had only been to the States once before, for a ballet performance in Houston when she was eleven. She barely remembered it. So we like to say she flew into the States for her first time on a private jet. She was so excited to finally see all of the places she'd always dreamed about, like Malibu and the Hollywood Hills and Las Vegas. And I couldn't have been more excited to show her my country. So we went on a tour. We stayed in Miami for two weeks, and then we headed to California, Las Vegas, and, finally, New York.

It was the end of October when we got back from our tour of the States, and I was hit with some bad news. I received a letter requesting $100,000 in damages from my first e-commerce partner. Because I had left him to start my own business, he was suing me for being in an apparent violation of our noncompete clause. *What the fuck?* I immediately called my attorney, Michael. He saw that the contract's jurisdiction was California, and told me noncompetes can't be enforced in California, because it's against state law. Thank God. He put that fire out fast, and I was free to do as I pleased in my e-commerce business. I never heard back from his attorney again. Now I was really fired up. It was time to go harder than ever on scaling my new venture with my partner Mike.

In December, Noemi and I went to Maui with my family for Christmas. I travel-hacked a three-bedroom villa at the Westin for only a few hundred a night. This was the same hotel I stayed at alone almost a year earlier when the pandemic struck. When we got back, Noemi decided she needed to go back to Spain and complete a task she'd left unfinished for too long: getting her driver's license. She'd never been able to get it, and it was making her crazy, especially since she's an actress and needs to be able to show her license to get almost all of her work. So once again, she flew home to Spain, and I stayed in Philly.

I was living with my roommates in my new home in the city, in the middle of winter, in the middle of the pandemic. Everyone was masked up and stuck at home. I ordered premade meals and just shut myself in the house. The universe once again had brought me back into a monk mode environment. Bitcoin had just broken its all-time high of $20,000, and I knew I needed more. The problem was my business cash flow wasn't coming in fast enough to keep up with the rising price of Bitcoin. So I decided to take a risk and took out a Bitcoin-backed loan with BlockFi. I put up ten bitcoins to be used as collateral and borrowed $100,000 against it. I immediately purchased $100,000 worth of Bitcoin (around five at the time) with the loan. This increased my portfolio value to over $500,000. I knew that I was going to become a millionaire in the next few months.

Since I had two other roommates paying for my mortgage and was cash flowing $500 a month profit, I decided there was no point in staying in Philly. Why not be in monk mode somewhere really nice? I realized I wasn't thinking abundantly, so I got the hell out of Philly and went back to Tulum by myself.

In Tulum, I decided to go on a thirty-day no-drinking challenge. Once again, I fell in love with Tulum. Something about living in the jungle made me feel so present. I felt connected with nature and was able to focus much more deeply on my work. I was sleeping like a baby, getting multiple hours of sunlight a day, reading books about Bitcoin and eating healthy, fresh seafood and grass-fed steak. Something inside of me told me to double down on Bitcoin even more. So I decided to take out another Bitcoin-backed loan with BlockFi, this time for $160,000, and with that loan, I purchased an additional five bitcoins. The BlockFi loans had secured me an additional ten bitcoins in total. And then, while I was there, on February 8, 2021, the announcement came out that Tesla had bought $1.5 billion worth of Bitcoin. Bitcoin had a massive 20 percent move, going from $36,000 to $46,000 in a single day. I looked at my BlockFi app and saw my portfolio read $1,200,000. I was officially a millionaire. Since I had been waking people up to Bitcoin on social media since it was under $10,000, I had tons of DMs from my followers thanking me for helping them discover Bitcoin. They were sending me pictures of their portfolios. Hundreds of thousands in gains, some even millions. It made me so happy. I had been right about Bitcoin and stayed disciplined, and it finally paid off.

I was generating multiple six figures a month in profit through my businesses by this time, so instead of paying down the principal of the loans, I kept buying more Bitcoin. Every week I received my wire from my e-commerce business or hit Payout on my Stripe account for Credit Class, and then I'd go on Coinbase Pro and smash buy. I was buying full bitcoins at a time, not even looking at the price. I was proud of myself for my discipline. I had Noemi in my life, so there was no need to waste money at clubs and on girls. I was traveling basically full-time, so I wasn't spending money on nice houses, exotic cars, or jewelry like everyone else on social media; I was just focused. My goal was set in stone: make as much money as humanly possible through my businesses and buy Bitcoin. In addition to the Bitcoin educational content I was making in Tulum, I also made my first video sales letter (VSL) for our Walmart automation service through my company with Mike. Prior to that, I hadn't had a video (or anything, really) explaining what the opportunity was, which meant I had to explain the same information over and over again each time I met a potential client. I was just posting stories and telling people to DM me if they wanted to get on a call. The process wasn't organized at all. I knew it was time to automate so I could buy more of my time back.

The VSL was one of the key things I created during this time. I built a system to automate my sales delivery. I created an explanation video where I went over the entirety of our services and talked about the differences between Amazon and Walmart automation. My buddy let me borrow his apartment in Tulum, and I got my camera and computer out and recorded screen shares of our current clients showing people what the stores and revenue stream breakdown looked like.

I explained everything: how much credit was necessary, the downsides, the risks, the pros and cons, and the expected ROI. I put it all into a nice twenty-five-minute video, and then I had my COO, Gavin, put it on the website. In addition to the VSL, visitors could also book a call directly through the site, and we integrated Calendly so the booking went right to my calendar. The requirements to book a call were that they had to watch the video to completion and write down all of the questions they had for me beforehand. I also took the time to schedule and film current client interviews and posted them on our website so potential new clients could learn more about the experience. Usually, they barely had any questions, since I'd already answered everything they could possibly ask in the VSL. My sales calls were less than ten minutes, and I'd close 80 percent of them, bringing in $35,000 to $40,000 a sale.

By doing this, I cut my work hours down by at least two hours a day. I no longer had to spend all day promoting my business. Now, people just saw me traveling the world and were like, "What the hell does this guy do?" They clicked the link in my bio, watched the explanation video, and booked a call if they had money to invest. Ninety percent of these people were ready to buy, and I hadn't even talked to them yet. It was mind-blowing. I was making more money than ever, and it just kept getting easier.

ELEVEN

THE UNIVERSE WILL PROVIDE

O NE NIGHT THAT WINTER WHILE I WAS STILL in Tulum on my own, I headed out to get dinner at a little taco shop I always go to. I passed by a tent on my way out of Nomade, and there was a sign that read Holotropic Breathwork Experience with Live Music.

I had no idea what that was, but I was curious, so I went into the tent. It was all lit up with candles inside, and a woman invited me to take a seat and lie down. I ended up doing this whole immersive breathwork experience for an hour straight.

It turns out that Holotropic Breathwork is a full spiritual experience, similar to DMT in some ways because you can have an out-of-body experience and can even experience an ego death, but there are no substances required. You access everything through the power of your breath. Some people connect with their inner child, some experience love and joy, and some just fall asleep. It's different for everyone.

I don't think I've ever experienced that much energy flowing through my body naturally—my hands, my feet, my heart. Afterward, I was completely free of all cravings and anxiety. I felt connected to something deeper. I asked the woman, "What did you just do? What *was* that?"

I took the woman, whose name was Onyay, to dinner that night and asked her to tell me everything about breathwork. I got so excited that I ended up asking her to help me organize a breathwork retreat on the spot. My followers were always so interested in my morning routine and my meditation practices, so I knew they would appreciate a spiritual-focused event, and I wanted to give back. The next day I made an Instagram story saying, "I'm hosting a breathwork retreat in Tulum! DM me if you're interested in coming," and BOOM, my DM's were flooded.

I started selling spots for $5,000 each. My new breathwork partner, Onyay, and I locked down a beautiful boutique hotel for our retreat and we set the dates for April.

Valentine's Day came and went, and spending it without Noemi sucked. I loved Tulum, but I couldn't wait to see her again. She had left for Spain at the beginning of January, and now it was almost two months later. That's a long-ass time. She hadn't even gotten her license yet, because she had to take an eight-week class before she could test for it. There was no way I was waiting another month. So I decided to fly her out to Punta Cana to meet.

Punta Cana was about halfway between us, and there was a direct flight from Spain. We stayed at an all-inclusive Hyatt for a week and did pretty much nothing except eat, drink, and lie out by the pool. When Noemi flew home, I prayed she would pass that damn test, and quickly.

I flew back to Philly and once again locked in on work. I knew by now that whenever I wasn't with Noemi I needed to sacrifice. I had so much motivation to experience the world and share my success with her. I always dreamed of being able to travel the world, but now I was able to share it with someone special.

Around this time, I also realized I needed to expand my audience and get more eyes on my content. That's when the idea popped in my head that I should focus on becoming more omnipresent. So I started a YouTube channel and created a TikTok account. I had watched Noemi film hundreds of

TikTok dances during our time together, but I always thought of the app as just a fun hobby. I decided I'd give it a shot and started posting Bitcoin/travel content daily on TikTok. The next trip I had planned was back to Dubai. I had always wanted to fly there first class on Emirates, and I finally had enough points to do it. On my first trip to Dubai, I'd only had enough points for business class, which was still awesome, but it wasn't first class, where you're literally drinking $1,000 bottles of champagne and ordering unlimited Michelin Star-quality food in your own private unit. Amex wanted one million points for the first class flight. Emirates only required 136,000 points. Because Emirates is a partner of Amex, I just transferred the points over to the airline through the transfer partners section. By doing this, I only had to cash in 136,000 points, which is equivalent to $1,360, instead of cashing in 1 million points, which would have been equivalent to $10,000.

I used the flight as an opportunity to blow up my new TikTok and shoot content of myself in my private suite: "This is what a $20,000 seat looks like! I got it for free with points!"

After enjoying caviar and champagne on the plane, I went to bed, and when I woke up my TikTok had gone viral with over one million views. I gained 25,000 followers just from that one video. I was so pumped. Once I got to Dubai, I got a room at the Marriott in the marina, and they upgraded me to the top floor of the building due to my Ambassador Elite status, which is the highest status you can get with Marriott. I ended up in a three-bedroom suite with two different balconies, one overlooking the bayside and the other overlooking the ocean, for only $140 a night.

While I was there, Bitcoin hit an all-time high of 64,000, and my portfolio shot up to $2 million with only $550,000 invested and $260,000 of that from the Bitcoin-backed loans. I couldn't believe it. Just a little over a year earlier, I was $50,000 in debt, and now I was sitting on $2 million worth of Bitcoin. I stayed in Dubai for almost a month, and Noemi finally joined me there after she passed her driver's license test. The international Marriotts are way more luxurious than the ones in the US, and they often come with lounges where food and drink are free, so Noemi and I definitely took advantage of that.

While we were there, we went on some outings from Dubai into the desert. We went sandboarding down sand dunes and rode dune buggies and camels, and of course I was shooting content the whole time for my Instagram. We even hired a local videographer with a drone to shoot some of our content.

In early April, I took Noemi to the St. Regis in Maldives. It was only a four-hour flight from Dubai, so it was easy. Hands down, this was the most beautiful place we'd ever been to. We had an overwater villa facing the sunset over the Indian Ocean. I used Marriott points to book the stay for free. We stayed five nights and had our own plunge pool on the deck. We did the same thing there that we do everywhere we travel. We work out every day, work a few hours, and then explore and have fun. I had finally become able to work anywhere in the world and live the life of a digital nomad.

From Maldives, the next big trip was back to Tulum, where I was holding the breathwork retreat. There were ten of us altogether, including me, Noemi, and my mom, and we did two two-hour sessions of breathwork every day for three days straight. It was a diverse group of people who signed up, and we all went very deep with each other and the bonds between us grew very strong. Every day, we'd work through our energy blocks with the breathwork, have emotional releases, and then sit in a circle and talk about it. By day three, everyone was crying and hugging each other. On the last night there, Noemi and I stayed up all night at a Black Coffee concert in the middle of the jungle, watched the sun come up, and swam in the ocean. I actually started crying because of how beautiful it all was. Noemi finally crashed, but I could not go to sleep. I decided to stay in the ocean, soaking in the beauty, and watched the sunrise over the Caribbean Sea. I took a moment to just celebrate my success. I felt so much love and compassion for myself and everything I had been through since I quit my job and began my journey. I had stayed consistent and sacrificed everything for my dreams, and they were finally coming true.

Noemi and I stayed in Tulum after the retreat for several weeks after the others from the retreat had gone home. After we left, Noemi and I looked at each other and wondered, *Now what?* We knew we wanted to travel all over Europe that summer, and after all of that travel in the spring, we felt like it was time to settle down for a while. We definitely didn't want to go back to Philadelphia or New Jersey. We didn't like the weather, the people, or the pace there. It was just not our scene, and I felt drained whenever I was there. I wanted to live somewhere that inspired me, somewhere that had no state tax, was full of entrepreneurs, and had beautiful weather year-round.

Miami was the first place that came to mind. We ended up renting a sweet Airbnb apartment on the seventieth floor of a high rise overlooking the Atlantic Ocean in Brickell. It was the tallest building in all of Miami and had the best views of the ocean and the city. Noemi and I both absolutely loved it. From the moment we got there, we felt like we were home. But the monthly rent was $12,000, which was outrageous. My goal was to stay there for a short period and then sign a lease on an apartment in the same building for more like $4,000 a month, which was the price they actually went for. But that would not be easy. Miami had gotten really crowded, and the real estate market was pretty impossible, mainly because so many people had flocked there during the pandemic to get away from the restrictions.

We settled in for the month in our overpriced Airbnb, and I went down to the leasing office and introduced myself to the leasing agent, but there was nothing available. Remember HACA? Hang up and call again? Well I applied the same method to the leasing office. I wasn't going to take no for an answer. I texted the woman in the leasing office every day to check on availability.

"Has anything opened up?" I asked, or "Sorry to bother you, but is there anything available yet?"

Sometimes I just texted her, and sometimes I went down to her office and said hello or brought her coffee. Meanwhile, Noemi and I meditated on this goal and visualized it every day, trying to manifest our apartment. We also said out loud affirmations every morning: "I am so happy and grateful now to wake up in our beautiful unit every day." We acted as if it was already done and we knew it would be done. But every day it was the same thing: nothing was available.

Bitcoin dropped all the way from $64,000 to $29,000 around this time. I was so convinced of its long term value that it didn't even bother me. I had studied the prior bull cycle of 2017 and knew that 50 to 80 percent drawdowns were common with Bitcoin, so I stomached it very well. And I wasn't overleveraged. I kept careful track of my loans and what the liquidation points were. I was prepared, because I had planned this out to include the possibility of the worst possible scenarios. I also had a lot of cash flow coming in from my businesses, so there were no problems there.

What I wasn't stomaching too well was the anxiety inside me. I think it had to do with staying in Miami for a while and not being distracted by traveling. I had a routine and a schedule, woke up regularly at a certain time every day, went to the gym, and then worked in our apartment. Settling down like this allowed me to realize that there was stuff bothering me; something was not settling right. So I decided to try to get to the bottom of it.

First, I invested into a men's entrepreneur group called Entrpreform, which was a community of men who helped each other become better in every aspect of life. I had seen other entrepreneurs post about their health habits: cold plunges, saunas, after-dinner walks, sleep hacks, and so on, and I knew that this would be a great place to invest my money.

I also came across another local Miami health legend around this time, Gary Brecka, and I signed up for a gene and blood test with his company, Streamline Medical. (This was right before he partnered with Grant Cardone.) After taking the tests, I had a lab review with a guy named Devin, who educated me about my health and prescribed natural medicine to reverse engineer my biochemistry and get all of my levels back to "normal." He said that with these few changes and additions to my new supplement stack, I would feel increased energy, sleep better, and experience zero anxiety. I was excited. I knew traveling full-time had taken a toll on my health, so I was ready to go *all in* on biohacking.

As I began to really dig into my mind and body, I realized I still had some anxiety from my past. I had never really thought much about getting assaulted at that party in New Jersey where I got my face smashed in and then getting drugged and pretty much kidnapped years later in Scottsdale. I mean, who knows? I'll never know what happened that night. I had just skipped over it, kept it out of my head, and kept on going. Now, I wanted to work through it so I could move on. There was still something going on. Even though I had all the success, I wasn't feeling 100 percent; I didn't have total peace of mind.

It was my twenty-fifth birthday around this time, and my COO, Gavin, had been researching a present for me when he came across Dr. George Pratt, who works with Rob Dyrdek and a bunch of other famous people. Dr. Pratt has been on Tony Robbins's show and a bunch of huge podcasts. He's all about clearing out negativity and past traumas, forgiving and forgetting the past completely, and how that leads to empowerment.

Gavin booked me an online session with Dr. Pratt as a birthday gift. We met on a Zoom call and over the course of two hours, he did all these things I'd never heard of, like tapping. I'm doing all these little finger taps, hitting all these points. I didn't even know what it was called. Now I know that the practice of tapping your fingertips on specific points of yourself is called EFT (emotional freedom technique) tapping.

I shared everything about my life with him: all the traumas, all the fucked-up shit, everything that was really bothering me and that I had never discussed with anyone besides Noemi a little here and there. Then he asked me to imagine one hundred balloons, each of which represented all of these traumas and problems. He had me put it all on the table, and we just threw it away through tapping and tossing invisible balloons in the sky. To be honest, I thought it was bullshit at the time. I wondered what the hell I was doing tapping my armpits and shit. But he was like, "You're gonna have to integrate this, but within three days, you're gonna feel it. Not tomorrow, but by day three, all this stuff is gonna be gone."

I thought, *Sure it is, dude.*

But he was not kidding. A couple of days later I woke up and suddenly felt limitless. From then on, I woke up totally free from anxiety. By that point, I was already working out with my trainer and eating extremely healthy. I was on Gary Brecka's supplement stack. My businesses continued to grow. Even though Bitcoin was dropping that summer, and I was watching my net worth get cut in half before my very eyes, I knew that everything was going to be okay. I finally released all the baggage in my life that I had been carrying around all that time. I finally confronted it and forgave myself, forgave everyone and everything that had happened. I let it all go.

It was a profound experience. Like, holy shit, who would've known this freaking dude in San Diego would be able to get on a Zoom call and cure my anxiety? But that shit worked. It really did.

One of the many amazing things that came out of working with Dr. Pratt was an increased connection with my higher purpose. I felt an enormous desire to give back after that. Since I had automated my credit course, and e-commerce was operated by Mike, I had a lot more free time on my hands. I wanted to create an opportunity to help more people.

One morning, shortly after the Zoom session with Dr. Pratt, I woke up at 4:00 a.m., startled by a big idea that had just swept over me. The download was basically this: I needed to make a new course. I needed to keep creating, and I needed to give back some value from what I'd learned over the past couple of years. This new course was going to be about much more than credit. It was going to be about the entire lifestyle I had leveraged: personal brand, credit, passive income, Bitcoin, and travel. That, in a nutshell, is the overview of what I went *all in* on next: my next signature course, Leveraged Lifestyle. I dropped the news of my plans on Instagram, and the reactions were extremely positive. There was a lot of excitement, and I knew this was going to be something that would help a lot of people have breakthroughs.

The next day was my birthday, and Noemi had planned a dinner at Papi Steak, which is my favorite restaurant in Miami. Jack and Ted were living in Miami by this point, and Noemi invited them. It had been a year since we'd last seen each other, so it was time. I ordered the restaurant's specialty: the Suitcase. It's a forty-eight-ounce Wagyu Tomahawk from Australia. When someone orders it, they shut down the whole restaurant, and then they do a light show as they bring out the meat. I'm telling you, if you're ever in Miami and have an extra $1,000 lying around, go to Papi Steak and order the Suitcase. You won't regret it.

Two days before we were set to leave for Barcelona, I went to Jeff Sekinger's Investor Con event in Miami, which was held on a massive yacht. People who I didn't know but who had been following my content came up to me to get their picture taken—with me. This had never happened to me before. I was blown away that people were actually starting to know who I was, and it gave me a sense of the impact of social media.

And then, the next day, Noemi and I were off to Barcelona. It was time to go back, because that's where my passion for travel had been born. I couldn't wait to be back in the place that changed my outlook on life, and to be there with Noemi instead of my college buddies. I knew it would be like I was seeing it for the first time all over again.

The goal had been to get an apartment lease in our building signed before we left for our trip. That way, when we got back home, we could move right in and we wouldn't have to worry about apartment hunting. I texted my friend in the leasing office the morning before we had to leave for the airport. "Sorry, Colin, I got nothing," she said.

We were so disappointed. I wasn't going to be able to text this woman every day from Spain, and we wouldn't have a place to live when we got back.

We got to the airport. Noemi and I were on a free flight, on standby. For standby, I always track all of the empty seats to project if I'm going to make it on a flight or not. But for some reason, I projected wrong that day. Noemi went to check us in, and the guy at the ticket counter told her, "The flight is full. You're not going to be able to board the plane."

I was pissed. I have never, ever missed a flight before, never screwed up the projections. I always got first class, too. But not that day. We headed back from the airport in an Uber, and I got us a hotel room at the W. There wasn't another flight for two days. I was livid.

The next morning we woke up to find a text from the leasing agent. "Colin! Are you still in Miami?"

I told her what had happened, and that we were leaving the next day instead. She asked me to come to the leasing office right away. A two-bedroom apartment had just opened up. It was the exact place we had visualized: a corner unit with a sunrise view of the ocean. We signed the lease immediately.

The universe had provided.

TWELVE

BUILD YOUR DREAM IN A MASTERMIND

THE DAY AFTER WE SIGNED THE LEASE, NOEMI and I successfully took off for Barcelona. We traveled all over Europe that summer, beginning with Barcelona, and then we were off to Ibiza.

I was still high off of the work I'd done with Dr. Pratt. I had so much creative energy flowing through me again and no blocks. I had all of this inspiration and was getting all of these signs that I needed to get busy creating my new course. While I was in Spain, I had a call with Brad Lea, who owns a company called Lightspeed VT, which specializes in teaching businesses how to create world-class learning systems. If you've ever taken Grant Cardone's Cardone University course, it's hosted on Lightspeed VT. It's an interactive course company with a platform that allows educators and influencers to create training modules, interactive courses, and anything else that has to do with learning online.

On our call, we discussed putting together my new course, Leveraged Lifestyle. As we developed it, I was able to implement the interactivity to customize the course for different types of individuals according to their different situations, kind of like a Choose Your Own Adventure format. For example, if you have a credit score of 700 or higher, you click on the left button and go down that path. If not, you click on the button on the right.

Brad is highly respected and popular in the industry, and he was not cheap. But since I was making good money by then, I wanted to put a lot of money into this course and make it really solid. I also hoped that if I shot this course with Brad, he would have me on his podcast, which receives over a million downloads per month. When we were first getting to know each other, Brad asked me about the e-commerce. "What are these Walmart stores?" he wanted to know. He seemed intrigued by the concept. I explained it all to him and told him that the Walmart stores cost $30,000. When I realized that was exactly what his services were going to cost, I asked if he wanted to swap. It turned out to be another strategic partnership and another win-win situation.

When Noemi and I were done traveling, we had a little setback heading back to the US. It was mid-July 2021, and Europe was not fully open to travelers. Spain was especially bad, and on the way back, we found out Noemi couldn't land in the States until she had quarantined for two weeks first in an approved country. She flew to Mexico to quarantine there for two weeks, while I flew to Miami to move us into the new apartment. We agreed to meet up again in Mexico once I'd finished the move-in.

I did an Instagram deal with some movers in Philadelphia and had all of our stuff moved to our new Miami apartment for only $2,000. I moved everything in, unpacked for the next five days, and then flew to Tulum, where we stayed for a week to finish out Noemi's quarantine before flying back to America together.

August 3, 2021, was a very big day: I met up with Brad Lea in person in Las Vegas. Since my COO, Gavin, lives in Havasu, and he and I had never met, even after being business partners for almost a year, he drove out to Vegas, and we all worked together to create the course. We got a nice suite and spent three days there working on it. The first day, we shot the course for twelve hours and got all of our footage. Then Brad's team went into the studio to edit and compile the course, based on the Five Pillars of the Leveraged Lifestyle: Personal Brand, Credit, Passive Income, Travel, and Bitcoin. As I hoped, Brad also invited me onto his podcast the next day. We got about thirty new clients just from that exposure, which was massive.

After that, Noemi and I went back to Spain for her sister's wedding in Marbella. Marbella is a vacation town on the coast, filled with villas, beautiful restaurants, and beach clubs. A friend of mine owns a couple of vacation homes there, and he offered to rent one to me for a couple of weeks for half price. It was awesome. While we were there, we hosted Noemi's family several times. Her sister had her bachelorette party there, and we also hosted a barbeque for Noemi's birthday and invited all of her friends and family, so I got to meet everyone. Her family isn't well off, so they were blown away when they walked into this insane villa that was really a mansion. I felt like they could see that Noemi was in a good place and being well cared for, which felt great. We swam and cooked and just got to know each other. It was an incredible experience.

Now. I know this book is about my life, but it wouldn't be complete without a chapter dedicated to someone who is a perfect example of the *go all in* mentality: my partner in crime, Noemi Hopper.

Noemi and I have both been growing and evolving ever since we got together. I know I have definitely changed for the better, and she also has been growing into her fullest, highest possible self. The definition of a mastermind is when two or more people come together to support and encourage each other, hold each other accountable, set high goals, and, more importantly, achieve them. I truly believe that that is exactly what our relationship has done for both of us.

When Noemi and I met up in Tulum that spring of 2020 and started falling in love, she was still trying to find her professional direction. She met my credit repair friend and partner Daryll there, and they really connected. In fact, they ended up working together on a network marketing company called TLC, which stands for Total Life Changes. This is a health and wellness company that sells liquid vitamins and weight loss products. Noemi worked really hard at that for a year, until she realized it wasn't a great fit for her. At the time, all of her audience was in Spain, and the products took three weeks to ship abroad. Also, they didn't have the support or customer service in Spain that was necessary for success. After a year doing network marketing for TLC, she decided to go back to her creative work—acting, dancing, and art. That is who she is at heart, so she went *all in*.

By mid-2021, Noemi had learned how to grow her Instagram, create stories, and cultivate an audience. She did well selling social media growth for a while (I passed her the torch) and then used that money to invest in her acting career. She went to New York and met the acting coach she had always dreamed of working with, joined his one-year program after the New York masterclass, and flew out to Los Angeles on her own dime, networking with a friend we had met in Tulum to stay at his house for free. She wanted to do this all on her own and wouldn't let me contribute anything toward it.

Los Angeles was a disappointing experience for her. It was nothing like what she had dreamed about: homeless people everywhere, ridiculous COVID-19 restrictions, and no in-person auditions. Everything was on Zoom. She went to LA thinking that she was going to find her big break but came back hopeless. She told me, "I'm not sure this is for me; I hate LA, which is the only place I can be if I want to pursue acting, and the industry feels so hostile."

I encouraged her to never give up. I reminded her of my story and how the universe will always test your willpower to see if you can keep going. You have to prove to it how bad you want it. I knew deep down that she had the talent to be an actress, and she knew it too. So she kept marketing herself as an actress in Miami on social media. Late in 2021, her impressive online presence paid off. One day, a private Instagram account with only 300 followers sent her a DM: "Hi, How are you? I'm a TV producer and I'm holding auditions for a Disney+ series. Would you like to participate?"

She thought, *Wait. What? This is somebody making a joke. There's no way Disney+ would contact me like this.* It was sketchy, but she wasn't taking any chances. After messaging back and forth, she realized that the casting office was in Miami, so if she did get the role they'd be shooting literally in our backyard.

They invited Noemi to send a selftape to audition for the show. After the audition, she had to wait to see if she got the role or not. She waited and waited for a month and heard nothing. Then finally, she got a callback. This time, she had to go in person and audition in front of more people. When she got out of that room, she knew immediately she had nailed it.

She came home and told me, "I'm not sure if I booked the role, but I definitely booked the room. My energy was so high. I was making them laugh, and I think they loved me."

I also had a gut feeling she was going to get this. But, of course, we had to wait again. This time it was only two weeks before she got the call. And then while she was working out at the gym her phone started ringing. It was the producer. Her heart was about to explode.

The producer said, "Hi, Noemi! The project will be recorded in late January, for about a month. We're starting rehearsals the second week. I'm still checking on the payment…"

She replied, "But wait, did I get it? Does this mean I got it? Or…"

And the producer said, "Oh yes! Congratulations, it's yours!"

She almost broke her arm throwing the weights on the floor. The whole gym was sure she was a psycho.

I am super excited to share that Noemi has a part on a new Disney+ series called *4EVER* that stars the Latin boy band CNCO. They're like the One Direction of South America. Noemi got the role because of her talent, no question about that. But we have to acknowledge that Disney never would have found her if she hadn't also learned about social media growth and put time and effort into growing her personal brand as an actress and dancer.

"I can't believe this," Noemi said to me the day we found out the role was hers. "I've been with a super famous manager in Spain since I was sixteen and never booked anything like this. Two months ago I grew my brand, and now I'm going to work for Disney!"

There was just one little glitch. She was still a Spanish citizen and needed a green card to be legally employed by the studio. Her ESTA Visa Waiver was about to run out, and she had only three days to get that proof of citizenship in order to keep the job.

We realized that if she could show proof that she was married and that her green card was on the way, she'd be fine. We love each other like crazy, so it was a no-brainer. The wedding? It was straight out of a fairy tale. In fact, it was right after our wedding that I realized I needed to write this book.

Within three days I got an attorney to draw up agreements about my businesses, and then we got married. Inside the FedEx Office. All the employees just stared at us as we became Mr. and Mrs. Yurcisin in our flip-flops. Actually, we didn't actually become Mr. and Mrs. Yurcisin—she will never give up her last name of Hopper, so technically it's Noemi Hopper Yurcisin. After we were married, I made her the majority owner of one of my LLCs and created a business bank account. We got all that over to Disney within the three days, and she shot the show. It's going to be a massive hit worldwide; I just know it.

The larger point here is that Noemi manifested her dream into reality, and she is literally the happiest I've ever seen her. She built her identity, and it solidified. She always knew she was an actress, and now she's proved it. She also has a massive audience on TikTok with over 700,000 followers and 10 million likes.

Here's what I have learned from my relationship so far with Noemi: I found her only when I truly started to love myself. Once I was on my right path and was happy with what I was doing, then and only then could Noemi come into the picture. And Noemi was at the same point in her life. She had given up a toxic relationship and was focused on getting to know and love herself. Then and only then can a relationship work: when two people who love themselves and love the path they're on combine their energies and support each other. There's no room for jealousy or fear about the other. And that's the only way a healthy relationship can be born.

You learn from your mistakes, celebrate your achievements, and build a relationship together based on respect and communication. That's what takes you to the next level. I wouldn't be the man I am today without Noemi.

THIRTEEN

TEN TAKEAWAYS

1. FIND YOUR PURPOSE

WAS SOLD ON "THE PATH" THAT EVERYONE WAS SUP-
posed to take. I was going to go to college, join a fraternity, and party. Everyone in my high school was sold on
the same dream. I never considered picking up my camera and starting to post on YouTube again. I was not in touch
with myself or my creative side at all. I had no intuition—or
at least I didn't pay attention to it. I didn't meditate. I was
just going with the flow, along with everyone else. I didn't
realize at the time that I had lost myself. I found myself again

through destroying my credit and rebuilding it. That was the moment when I realized I could make money helping people and having a positive influence on the world. The feeling surpassed anything I had felt before; it was pure joy. I had found my purpose.

2. FOLLOW YOUR BLISS

If I learned one major lesson from my college years, it was this: if you follow your bliss, it will lead you not just to happiness but also to success. Traveling to Barcelona was just the beginning for me. It was the launching point from which I would slowly start to build my dream life...a life filled with freedom and happiness, love and success, and, of course, travel. You don't have to be in a meeting. You don't have to be at work. You can be on a boat in the Mediterranean, having fun, and if you keep your eyes open, you might meet someone who will change your life and change your business. Because every day is work and every day is play.

3. THE MORNING ROUTINE

Developing my morning routine was one of the most transformative experiences I have ever had, and I believe it is one of the most transformative experiences *anyone* can have. It had a huge impact on me—in fact, you could say it directly led to my successful career as an entrepreneur. If I hadn't started the morning routine, I would have never come to know how close I was to being able to quit my job, or how much money I could make on the side, or how to make content or set goals. I wouldn't know any of that.

4. LISTEN TO YOUR GUT

I am living proof that if you have the courage to listen to your inner voice, things will always work out. The definition of success is different for everyone, but one thing applies to us all: if you listen to your intuition, you will find success. Over and over, life has shown me this. When I listen to it, I move toward happiness, and when I don't, well, I don't.

5. FORM STRATEGIC PARTNERSHIPS

Often, we choose people who are not really good for us. They may seem like amazing people at first; we may be impressed with their marketing glitz and the look of it all, but a lot of people are not really what they seem. So one of the keys to our success, ultimately, is getting wise about whom we choose to trust with our business and, of course, with our money...and learning to let them go when it doesn't work out. Making the shift toward people who were trustworthy and aligned with my core values is what made a huge difference for me. My COO, Gavin, is a great example. He helps me work smarter, not harder. Do I want a website? He sets it up. Do I need something automated? He handles it. Virtual assistant? Boom. Done.

6. YOUR NETWORK IS YOUR NET WORTH

A huge part of going *all in* is making connections with people. Because I believe that you become a version of the five people you hang out with the most, I cannot stress enough the value of networking. If I hadn't started going to networking events, I don't know if I would have ever gotten my business off the ground, much less watched it soar over the last couple of years. Today, I'm hosting my own networking events. I'm the person speaking and bringing in speakers. But, way more importantly, I'm helping people. What they say really is true: your network is your net worth.

7. KNOW YOUR VALUE

In Bali, when I had lost all momentum and sales were down, I kept pushing, kept persevering, kept dropping those videos. And eventually, I had momentum again. One sale led to another, and then they were trickling in again. Whenever someone bought my course, I'd take a screenshot and post it on my story. This made people react and think, *Oh, he's buying? Damn, maybe I should buy, too.* It's basic marketing—we can entice people to buy just by getting them to watch other people buy. You have to realize your value, believe in what you have to offer, and take nothing personally. When you decide on a price point, never lower it; only make it higher.

8. LEARN THE LESSON IN EVERYTHING

As much as I hated working for ADP, it taught me tricks of the trade that directly fed my ability to make my online businesses successful. For instance, it trained me to use touchpoints—tracking how many times I reached out to a buyer. This data helped me stay on top of the follow-up game with my own businesses. Wrestling, which I also hated, gave me the discipline to become the entrepreneur I am today. It's how I learned to really push myself and never give up. When I wrestled, I could throw up in a trash bag from the workout and then four minutes later run right back onto the mat to finish another hour of practice. That's where I developed the mindset that I still use today in my business: I can get through anything. Even when you're not where you want to be—yet—you need to be grateful for what you're gaining from the experience.

9. THINGS HAPPEN FOR YOU, NOT TO YOU

Getting booted out of Cabo was the best thing that ever happened to me. To this day, I know for a fact I would be dead if I'd spent that week in Cabo. I would have drunk my kidneys and liver into failure. I would have poisoned myself, because that acne medicine is powerful and nothing to mess with. At that moment, my connection to something bigger than myself took hold. I cried out of gratitude and thanked God. From that moment on, whenever significant events took place, instead of *reacting*, I learned how to stay calm, ask why this was happening, and then *respond* to it.

10. JUMP INTO FEAR

On the other side of fear, something amazing is always waiting, so keep building that muscle by jumping into fear. What's the worst thing that can happen? You get rejected. Congrats! You are right back to where you were before. You didn't lose anything; you just gained experience. There were so many times I said no to the more logical choice and jumped into fear. Like quitting my job, flying Noemi and her friend across the world to meet me, and helping my mom retire when I was just twenty-four years old. These scary decisions turned out to be some of the most fulfilling things in my life. On the opposite side of fear, the best version of yourself is waiting.

CONCLUSION

You'll never know how far your impact will go. On that fateful day in 2019 when I left my corporate job in Scottsdale to go *all in* on the entrepreneurial life, I had no idea how it was all going to turn out. All I knew was that I had to do it.

This book was written out of my desire to document that journey in writing so that anyone, anywhere could follow along and see that it can be done, no matter the circumstances. My goal with these pages has been to inspire you to start your own journey. Some of the lessons I've learned have been harder than others. Terrible, scary things happened to me, or rather, for me, before I decided to make massive changes in my life, but it was those awful things that rerouted me back to my right path. I encourage everyone to see those roadblocks and pitfalls as signs to wake up. All you need is one sign that really resonates with you to begin.

In my late teens and very early twenties, I fell off the path that I should have been on the whole time. I abandoned my innate creativity and cared too much about what others thought. When I was seven, I was creating books for my family and immersed in building original creations with Legos. And then I picked up a skateboard and a camera, and I kept on creating. But then, because my environment did not support those activities and I felt like an outcast, I ignored what my heart was telling me. I decided I should just play sports, go to college, and get a job. Well, I tried that, and I was miserable. Staring up at the ceiling on that creaky bed in that stinky Scottsdale Airbnb, nursing another hangover, I knew there was so much more out there for me. There had to be.

I know by now that my deepest sense of fulfillment is in my work. Don't get me wrong; the travel, the money, the freedom, and all that stuff is great. But I promise you, there is no better feeling than empowering someone to change their life. That all comes from the work you put out into the world. Your "work" can come in many forms: a course, a podcast, an article, a TikTok, an Instagram, a YouTube, a tweet, or a book. As long as you're adding value to others' lives, I consider that work. The more work you do the more fulfillment you'll have. That's why I wrote this book. I'm not falling for the materialistic traps. I'm not here for instant gratification.

I know my purpose is to help people. I don't care how long it takes. Or how hard it is. I know that this book is going to change lives. I understand that this book will make me want to write a second, and then a third, a fourth, and so on. I know this book will get me on more stages, podcasts, and interviews. This is just another piece of my work. And I've created it with the intention to make the world a better place.

If you are on the crest of taking the plunge yourself, jump into your own fear, and go *all in*. The possibilities are endless, if you only believe in yourself and allow yourself to take some risks.

Maybe when you were a kid, you loved to sing. But one time, someone made fun of you in school. You felt horrible. After that, every time you sang, you worried that it was the wrong thing to do. Your peers and your parents thought you were silly, so you stopped. Instead, you went off and did everything everyone said you should.

That was then. Now, hopefully—maybe even after reading this book—you wake up. Something resonates with you, and you realize you have the power to decide.

Most people just wander through life without waking up to what the universe wants them to do with their lives. If this is you, if you feel lost and like something is missing, I hope this book has helped you shine a light on what that is. I hope that you feel empowered and realize no one can do this but you. Find what ignites you and go after it.

The most important thing about this story is to follow your heart and your gut. Once you do that, everything will fall into place. You will know that your network is your net worth because you will be drawn to people who are doing what you want to do and you will listen to that intuitive attraction. You will be able to jump into your fear because you will be too excited to stay complacent and safe. You will know that things happen for you, not to you, because each significant event has a lesson you were meant to learn. You will be able to go for it because you will have nothing to lose but your misery.

You will see that credit is key because the world runs on debt, and it unlocks so many of the imaginary doors between you and your goals. You will come to see that the universe always provides, and you will enter into relationships that feel like masterminds, because you finally love yourself enough and would only choose somebody who will value you as much as you value yourself. I wish you courage, peace, and joy on your own personal journey of going *all in*.

And never forget to enjoy the ride.

—Colin Yurcisin

FINAL THOUGHTS

I want to take this time to say thank you to everyone who's been involved in my journey so far.

Mom and Dad, I would not be the man I am today without you. I seriously could not have been raised by better parents. Your unconditional love has been there for me through the entire journey. Mom, thank you for always giving me so much love and instilling kindness in me, and Dad, thank you for pushing me to never quit anything in life. Thank you for sticking together through thick and thin, your marriage, and the way you raised me, Kylie, and Caitlyn. That is something to be so proud of. I love you guys.

To my little sisters, Kylie and Caitlyn, I love you guys so much and I am so grateful to have you in my life. You guys motivate me to be better. I can't wait to watch you two grow up and achieve your dreams.

To my grandparents: Mommom, Grandma, Grandpa George, Memmom, thank you for all of your love and support and contributing so much to my college education. I wouldn't have gotten the experience I needed without you guys. To all of my extended family members who have shown me love and support.

To my boys I grew up with—Jack, Richard, Justin, Eric, Connor, Sam, Mark, Zach, Alex, and Brandon—thank you for everything. I will never forget the time we spent together during middle school and high school. Growing up with you guys, and experiencing life for the first time with you all, was so pure, and so exciting. I will always be there for you guys, even though we don't get to see each other as much anymore.

To the friends I met in college, Harrison, Zach, Ben, Marco, Sam, Jake, Bryce, and Trent: What an unbelievable experience we shared together. A movie could be made about our college experience. Those were easily some of the most fun times I've ever had, even though most of it is a blur. I'll always be here for you guys and I'm excited to reconnect.

To Pauly: If it weren't for you, bro, I wouldn't be where I am today. Our friendship carried us through the trenches of the many rude awakenings entrepreneurship had in store for us. I seriously don't know what I would have done without you, especially in those times we both wanted to quit. Thank you for forgiving me. I am so happy to call you a brother and I am so proud of you for everything you've accomplished. I will always be here for you, no matter what.

To Jack and Ted, I knew the day I met you guys that you were going to be successful in whatever you did in life. Jack, I'm so proud of you for everything you've been able to accomplish with your love for business credit, and I'm so glad our paths crossed and that I could be the one to introduce you to it. Ted, I'm so proud of you for going in your own direction and pursuing your dreams in fitness. I'll never forget the laughs we shared together in that Hawaii house.

To Connor, my childhood best friend and now my business partner in our mining company, Leveraged Mining, it feels like a dream to have a business with you. From all the hours of us listening to podcasts about business while working the assembly line at your dad's company to now finally owning a business together…dreams really do come true.

To my content creation team Matt, John, and Shahab, thank you guys for helping me push my message to the masses on a daily basis. I can't wait to smash 100,000 subscribers on YouTube and then 1 million! My brand would be nothing without you.

To Gavin, you're always someone I can count on. You've been loyal and committed since day one, and I thank you for everything you've done. To many more years of success.

To Francis, from meeting you in that random New Jersey backyard ten years ago at that Vemma event to now being best friends, traveling together, and buying real estate together, you've always been there for me, and I appreciate you for everything.

To Noemi, since you've come into my life everything has gotten better. You were with me from the beginning, and I credit so much of my success to you. I can't even put into words how much you mean to me. Experiencing everything with you by my side has been a dream. I love you so much, and I can't wait to experience all of our wildest dreams as they come true with each other.

To you, reader: Thank you for reading this book. Nothing would be possible without the love and support you've shown for me. I thank you for being a part of my journey.

Printed in Great Britain
by Amazon

45467378R00148